The Coming Storm

The Coming Storm

Its cause and background

Murdoch Campbell

Edited by David Campbell

Covenanters Press

Covenanters Press
an imprint of
Zeticula Ltd,
Unit 13,
196 Rose Street,
Edinburgh,
EH2 4AT,
Scotland.

http://www.covenanters.co.uk
admin@covenanters.co.uk

First published 1948

This edition published 2016
Text © David Campbell 2016

Front cover: *The Soutars of Cromarty* © Donald M. Shearer
Back cover: *Storm Effects – Ben Ledi* © H. Morley Park

ISBN 978-1-905022-40-3

Contents

Our God shall come, and shall not keep silence: a fire shall devour before him, and it shall be very tempestuous round about him. (*Ps.* 50: 3)

Mary Campbell, née Fraser, c. 1925.

Preface

On a fair summer morning, years ago, the writer travelled through Highland scenes in the company of a distinguished scholar of evangelical outlook. In conversation he ventured the question, "If you were a Christian minister, what theme would you most emphasise in these times?" The scholar answered, "The Biblical doctrine of evil, of course. We should always remember that the whole of Revelation, as well as God's actions in time, are intimately related to the presence of evil in the world." That was all. The view from the train window was too enchanting to dwell further on such a dark subject. Two years later the writer jotted down in tentative form the substance of what now appears on the following pages. This he did, after reading such books as *Must Destruction Be Our Destiny?* by Dr. Harrison Brown, and after giving a measure of thought to the moral situation in our contemporary world. He no longer doubts that this nuclear age of moral collapse and grave religious decline has brought us to the brink of a chasm from which it seems impossible to retreat. We lack both the spiritual power and the moral resource to do so.

This booklet offers a word of explanation that may help us to understand the background of the present ominous hour in the life of this planet. It is meant to serve as a red light which might prepare some fellow wayfarers for the coming disaster. It might also lead them to pray that the God Who rules the nations might still work a miracle of mercy to prevent what we fear is so imminent. His will be done.

Chapter I

Evil emerging

SURFACE WAVES

1. Cain

He was a powerfully built man. His splendid physique, developed by his diligent attempt to extract a living from the sullen soil, bore the stamp of mature manhood. He was, in fact, the first man who ever entered this world through the mystery of conception and birth. Because something had happened in the life of both his parents he was "born in sin and shaped in iniquity"—a potential moral monster. For some inexcusable cause his younger and sweet-natured brother became the subject of his incurable malevolence.

They are alone now, his brother and he. Apart from Abel's flock the whole Syrian plain is quiet and uninhabited. The world is still young and noiseless. No eye could see the deed or discover the grave—the first grave ever opened. Something swept over the man's mind, and for the first time in history the loud cry of instinctive fear rent the air, and broke the sweet silence which gave such unutterable dignity to this world. It sounded like the opening bar of a song composed in hell, as in fact it was. The grave is covered. A terrifying new shadow rested on the murderer's mind. It was guilt. He heard an accusing Voice speaking to him from Heaven, and from within himself.

Many centuries afterwards a man wrote a wonderful letter in which he asked the question, "Wherefore slew he him?"

2. Noah

The years pass. If we had lived then we could have heard a strange medley of many noises, a weird confusion of song, shout and scream. God Himself describes it as 'violence' and 'corruption', which in modern language means vandalism, bloodshed, immorality, drunkenness and theft. It is 'the modern way' in the old antediluvian world. The physical giant and the facile female who shares his licentious conduct are unashamed. He is a moral degenerate. So is she. The woman is not his own wife, for the sacred institution of marriage is long since unobserved. Only a few insufferable 'Puritans' worry over those breaches of a supposedly Divine ordinance. Night falls. The stars shine in their remote purity. The nocturnal promiscuous revel is just beginning. Why should they not abandon themselves to every form of sensual indulgence? Night throws its mantle of concealment over the whole lurid scene. All moral law had been murdered the night before, and would be murdered again this night.

There is one jest which never fails to amuse. The eccentric, lonely shipbuilder who lives among them, and who has been telling them about the coming judgment of flood for nearly two hundred years, had made no convert outside his own home. His gigantic ship is the joke of the century. The sun rises over the hills of Mesopotamia. In the distance they hear the sound of a hammer. Noah is up early. God's heart is grieved in Heaven, and His lips have spoken the just but fateful words: 'I will destroy man'. His instrument of destruction is ready. The skies darken with startling suddenness. It is beginning to rain. . .

3. Egypt

The man who hurries along those ancient lanes is the prophet of Jehovah. He might have wondered at the severity of God in His actual and threatened judgments. God would therefore have him see a little of the hideous, hidden 'abominations' which had offended 'the eyes of His glory'. By a subtle, serpentine movement something strange and forbidden had entered the very Temple of God. With inaudible step God leads him towards

His House. There is present a congregation of seventy, practising in deep secrecy what was in effect an Egyptian High Mass. The lights are low, for it is a work of darkness.

"I went in and saw every form of creeping things. . .and all the idols of the house of Israel. . .Every man had his censer in his hand. . .Then said He unto me, Son of man, hast thou seen what the ancients of Israel do in the dark? . . .for they say, The Lord sees us not; the Lord hath forsaken the earth". To them (in the language of modern blasphemers) God was "dead".

The invisible Hand leads him away that he might see 'greater abominations': 'women weeping for Thammuz'. It is 'Passion Week', the weird rite of ancient idolatry and of a perverted Christianity. These men had succeeded in bringing to maturity, by an imitation of heathen practice, the greatest spiritual perversion known to man—the displacement of joy and hope through 'glad tidings' for a dismal sinful sorrow of which both the religion of Israel and apostolic Christianity knew nothing. It is a sorrow similar to that of fallen spirits who tremble because Christ came, died, and rose again, and by these His mighty acts forever frustrated their designs, destroyed their works, and triumphed over them on His Cross. Between this 'weeping' and the wholesome repentance of the people of God there can be no comparison; God in His Word recognises none.

The prophet again is led to witness what came to be known as the scene of the eastward pose. To those who practise it, it is a gesture attractive to the eye, and poetic in its significance; but God saw in it a total rejection of His Word, and a defiance of His will. These abominations have persisted through the centuries, and are being enacted and brought to maturity in this age, and with infinitely greater aggravation, on the banks of both the Tiber and the Thames. Not only in Rome but in Canterbury.

4. Calvary

It is late. The hush of night is fallen on the whole land. These men would have been asleep also except for the urgent business on hand. They had just sent away a party to apprehend a 'wanted' Man. In the light of a candle they glance furtively at one another—waiting. This is their hour of revenge. They are 'high Churchmen', and their motives in what they are about to do are really, they claim, in the interests of national security and religious conformity. There is the sound of footsteps outside. The party have returned, and they have the Prisoner. Good! A verdict is reached. The sentence of death is pronounced, and they know how to carry it out in its most painful and ignominious form. Morning comes. They stand on the edge of a crowd studying hard every word and every move of the man on the balcony. He is a Roman, and has the last word in this case; but that word, come what may, must agree with theirs. They had already in the darkness of the night broken the Laws of God and man in their letter and spirit. They would force this Roman to do the same. The subtle and well-chosen weapons in their armoury they would use as the need arose to override all arguments and resistance. 'Pilate could avail nothing.' They must have His blood to spill, and His flesh to tear. Again night falls, but it falls in the middle of the day. Nature in sympathy with its Incarnate God would, if it could, conceal His shame and His last agonies as, in our nature, He gives up His spirit on the Cross of Calvary.

What was His crime? None. He merely went about doing good. He healed the sick, fed the hungry, and raised men from the dead. He preached the world's greatest sermon, and lived it to perfection. His very breath purified the world, as His blood redeemed it. 'They hated Me without a cause.' Who was He? Let us leave the answer to this question to the ONE Who knew Him better than any other. 'But unto the Son He saith, Thy throne, O God, is for ever and ever.' God's only, eternal, Son.

Let us ask a deeper and a more difficult question. Did they know? Was this wholly done in ignorance, or was it a case of sheer enlightened malevolence in its eternal opposition to recognised and absolute Goodness? Did they sin against knowledge? While we know that some committed this great evil ignorantly, and in unbelief, it is also profoundly significant, as our Lord predicted in His parable, that not until all doubt and questioning were resolved did they say, "This is the Heir: let us kill Him'.

Men do not always sin in ignorance even in this higher sphere of moral conduct, which involves destiny itself. There is, for example, nothing more obvious in the modern world than that a studied and similar attempt is made to dethrone Christ as 'Lord of Lords', and to break His authority as Head of His chosen and redeemed Church. The Second Psalm might have been written an hour ago.

5. Fascism

We are surrounded by a baffling pile of architecture. Somewhere within this stupendous mass of masonry a small white-robed figure sits in a small room. The flowing white robes and other personal adornments are hardly able to conceal the wrinkled ferocity of his face. His name is 'Pope Innocent III'. On the desk before him is a gorgeously coloured parchment which has to do with a 'sect' who live in the quiet Alpine valleys. They have committed a great crime. Having read their Bible they now refuse the teachings of the Roman Church. The multi-coloured parchment has to do with their destruction. The Crusade is actually under way, and already about one million men, women, and children have perished.

Three centuries pass. The Pope—a different person, but animated by the same spirit—is still at his desk looking at columns of figures. It is gratifying that in forty years 900,000 'heretical elements' have been disposed of under the irrevocable curses of the Church. It soon became the most expert gravedigger in Europe and, considering its primitive means of destruction, its achievements in this sphere of mass murder are without compare.

Again the centuries pass, and the year is 1939. The world has changed, but the Church is 'always the same'. The white-robed figure is still in his room. Popes perish, but the human link in 'the apostolic succession' is maintained. Before him lie two concordats—the ripe fruit and the grand result of much negotiation with two 'Catholic soldiers', Benito Mussolini and Adolf Hitler. Should the deluge of blood let loose on the world end in favour of 'the Fascist powers' the Church, it was clearly understood, would have with their help a free hand in the elimination of all hostile 'non-Catholic' elements in Europe and beyond. This applied particularly to Protestant democracy as well as Russian communism. Which means, in all truth, that in this white-robed figure "we are dealing with ideas left over from the black ages in the brains of a being at once puerile, perverted and malignant", and that "before mankind can get rid of it the Papacy may drown our hope for the coming generation in a welter of blood, in an attempt to achieve a world-wide St. Bartholomew's Eve". We are dealing with more: with a form of incarnate evil parading in the high pretension of holiness and delegated divine authority within a system which many millions of deluded human beings call 'the Church', and which in this ecumenical age we are asked to acknowledge as the only true Church.

[*Mr Campbell attacks the 'pretensions' and 'delegated authority' of the Papacy, and its role in the Second World War. His attitude to Catholic people, however, could not differ more. His attack, and the language of his day, should not obscure his love for Catholics who have faith in Christ, and regard for their good deeds done in His name.* :- Ed.]

6. Blitz

Millions of wearied heads move uneasily on their pillows at an hour when 'this breathing world' should be resting peacefully in the kindly folds of night. The awakening to consciousness is accompanied by sudden mental pain, and a sickening apprehension of real danger. As the last note of warning sirens dies away a dull distant thud comes, like a reminder that death has driven its first nail into another gigantic coffin. The night becomes alive with a medley of hideous noises which suddenly grow in intensity. Brave men seek to compete with death as it rages in all its fury; but the task is almost hopeless. For those who must stand still, time, in its obstinate refusal to pass quickly, assumes the quality of eternity. An ambulance races through the streets. Inside, a young nurse lays her finger very gently on the diminishing pulse of a young mother, whose now lifeless child is covered in a corner. The child was born suddenly and prematurely after her home was demolished earlier in the night. They reach the hospital. An air raid warden puts up a discouraging hand as he points to an enclosure across the wrecked wall. 'A land mine got it only a few minutes ago', he explained. There is a running to and fro as silent men carry their burdens up to the terrace in the darkness. As the ambulance moves away, the nurse, with her fingers still on the pulse, whispers the words, 'She is gone: you may turn back'.

7. Ravensbrück

They poured in every day, a constant stream. Every head is bowed and the step through weariness and hunger is slow. A cruel, imitative voice commands a more erect posture, and a quicker pace. They are all women, of all ages. A strange, fantastic cloud is over the memory of most of them. Some remember, however, the black tragedy of past months. Or is it really the same world? If it is a wicked dream, when will morning come and the time to awake. . .? The straggling crowd reach the inner fence, and at last arrive at the place of horror. They call it 'Ravensbrück': the House of Death. It could and did accommodate 118,000 women—the wives, mothers, sisters, daughters and sweethearts of men many of whom are involved in ever worse terrors.

"There were also 600 children whom some of us carried into the camp in our wombs, but who perished before their eyes could see the day. They were taken out of our fleshless arms and carried across the way where the doctor did something to them. Only about 18,000 of us survived while the other 100,000 could not be accounted for. We could not tell whether it was mental death or despair which looked out from our eyes—those eyes which never seemed to close—or whether it was that the woman corporal muttered 'Ja' every day before a number of us who were removed later in the day. Nor could we understand how young women after seeing the doctor rapidly became old, wrinkled and grey. We heard later that 7,000 of us perished in the gas chamber."

One whose horrified eyes looked upon the scene wrote, "God give me the words to describe Ravensbrück. If I were the greatest painter, poet or orator I could not give a full picture." All this happened in Europe a few years ago.

8. Hiroshima

The clock is striking eight from the tower of Shinto in Hiroshima. Yet up in the remote blue sky there is a plane. In its historic belly it carries one bomb, and a man, after readjusting the beautiful silken parachute on which it is to glide ever so gently on this city of 250,000 souls, emitted in quiet tones the two words: 'Bomb gone. . .'

Down in the city a young widow was sitting reading her newspaper. The breakfast of rice was prepared, but her three children were still sleeping. For a few moments she watched the patriotic activities of a neighbour until she reacted in instinctive terror. There was a tremendous blinding flash of light across the sky as if a thousand mirrors had simultaneously flashed in the light of a hundred suns. She was instantly lifted off her feet and borne into the next room followed by parts of the house. She heard her five-year-old boy cry, 'Mother, help me', but the other two had vanished.

At that moment scores of thousands of human beings were swept to instant death, followed through the coming hours by many thousands of others who passed through the unutterable horrors of this first scientific experiment in thermonuclear warfare.

There was no sound heard in the city itself. Only 20 miles away a lone fisherman in his sampan, casting his net, heard the deafening reverberating roar as the bomb exploded. To those in the city it was silent, sudden destruction. Waves of shattered humanity congregated here and there with the last pitiful plea of 'a drink of water'.

The smoke of the city, mingled with a sullen cloud of dust, turned day into night. There was 'blood, fire, and vapour of smoke'. Literally speaking the sun was turned into darkness; and the night glow made the moon appear as if it had been bathed in blood. A raging typhoon added to the general horror. It was nature's way of reacting against the power which disturbed its beneficent rule in the air, which the blast of the bomb had forced outwards. This was followed by a deluge of rain which drowned many who were too weak to move to higher ground, out of the way of river floods.

In the ruins of the city a Christian minister is reading the Bible to a dying Japanese. A ray of light comes in through a hole in the demolished apartment where the man is dying. In its light he reads from the ninetieth Psalm.

You turn man to destruction; and say, Return, you children of men.
For a thousand years in Your sight are but as yesterday when it is past, and as a watch in the night.
You carry them away as with a flood: they are as a sleep: in the morning they are like grass which grows up.
In the morning it flourishes, and grows up: in the evening it is cut down, and withers.
For we are consumed by Your anger, and by Your wrath are we troubled.
You have set our iniquities before You, our secret sins in the light of Your countenance.
For all our days are passed away in Your wrath: we spend our years as a tale that is told.

It was a message not only for a dying heathen, but also for a sinful world to whom the wrath of God is revealed from Heaven.

These several and lengthened instances of wickedness and terror may well cause the reader to ask what is it all about.

We simply want to show that there is something very far wrong with man, and with the world because of man. Our

9

Chapter must end here as we cannot see the end. We can discern, however, that failing an amendment of manners, and a penitent return to God for mercy, another new and terrifying affliction is coming to man. For our generation the sun appears to be sinking fast in a stormy sea. Abounding iniquity is preparing a pathway for 'God's strange work', 'because a short work will the Lord make on the earth'.

Chapter II

Theories of sin

THE SHALLOWS

The question we now ask is: What is wrong with our world, and what is the cause of this destructive thing called 'sin' which produces these historical and impending agonies, a few of which we have mentioned, and which appears to be at the root of our temporal and eternal sorrows? The question is answered by God. It is also answered by man. But their witness does not agree. Man, especially within the last two centuries, has attempted, by manifold interpretations, to elucidate this problem. We fear, however, that his several theories have, more than anything else, been responsible for the successive 'breakdowns' in our moral standards, and for the several world disasters which have recently overtaken us. Let us see how he explains the presence of evil in this pained world.

1. Free choice

We may begin with coarser strands of thought, working our way upward toward more plausible, but equally unsatisfactory, suppositions related to this subject.

The lowest rung in the ladder is the modern view that since God is answerable for man's creation He is therefore responsible for his actions. Apart altogether from the moral insanity which this view contains we know that God created man both a sinless and a free being. He also blessed him with a fullness of power to resist evil should it come, and with a fullness of knowledge as to how it might be committed. He forewarned him of the wages which his sin would truly earn. He placed before his eyes in the Garden of Eden the mystic symbol of His will which was always to remind him that it was God's glory, as 'God over all', to command the creature, and that the glory of man consisted in a loving obedience to His Word. God's warning, we think, implied the prior existence of evil, and the possibility of its invasion upon his honoured state as created in God's image and favoured with His constant communion. Man's power to choose marked his highest dignity as a free moral being; but not, however, to choose what was contrary to God's will. That would only involve him in spiritual bondage, as it did, and in the awful loss of that perfect freedom which he enjoyed in His service. When man therefore sinned through the wilful forfeiture of his life and freedom, the responsibility was wholly his. He stands guilty and condemned at the bar of God. 'Wherefore thou art inexcusable, O man, whosoever thou art.'

2. The moral law

An equally disastrous view is that what we call the objective moral law, by which sin is revealed and forbidden, is only a theological fiction. This is one of the evil fruits of modern liberal theology. Some have even dared to preach that the Biblical Moral Law is nothing but a series of ancient 'Calvinistic "don'ts"', or a 'theological scarecrow' erected by a Jew 'to prevent us from enjoying life'. When accredited theological teachers relegate the first five Books of Scripture to the category of indifferent history, and when the phenomena associated with Revelation itself are dismissed as largely the tendency of a primitive nomadic mind to give supernatural colouring to natural events, it is not then surprising if one of the chief glories of the older dispensation— the communication of the Moral Law to mankind— should suffer from the reckless scepticism of modern times. The Law of God, however, bears the evidence on its own face that its origin is divine. It is not in man to write such words or think such thoughts. By its comprehensiveness and brevity it stands an everlasting proof of its divine origin. It is man's chief safeguard against the disintegrating power of evil. In this true mirror we see clearly what our duties toward God and men are. It is God's objective and authoritative standard by which human conduct is either condemned or praised. Being final and 'categorical' the transgression of it, or the omission to fulfil its precepts, is sin. For a moral world, a moral law is a necessity. Could anything be more absurd than to brand as 'fictitious' the subjection of man, as a moral being, to an appropriate and necessary moral law, while we must concede that every other creature in the universe, and the universe itself, are subject to law? Both the astronomical and atomic universes are under law. We have also a dread insight, in these modern times, into what the wilful violation of the laws governing the physical universe may mean for man. Though the analogy is not perfect, we may say that if the invasion of the fundamental laws which govern the material universe may mean the end of our civilisation, including the destruction of our own bodies, will not the persistent violation of the Law which is the 'basic substance' of all moral existence involve us in spiritual death and irrevocable disaster? There is, in fact, no escaping this conclusion.

3. Conscience

Those on the other hand who follow an uncertain subjectivism, and who deny the existence of any moral law except that which is implanted in our own mind, make sin to consist simply of going against one's conscience—'the moral law within'—and in being unfair to our own moral sense. If we are true to the light which is in us, it matters not how we stand in relation to the letter or the spirit of the Moral Law written in the Bible. This is the philosophy which teaches that 'every man is entitled to his own opinion' and should follow 'the way that seems good to him'. This, of course, is but the thoughtless language of those of old who, when left without a king, did that which seemed right in their own eyes. When the great John Knox discovered that Mary Queen of Scots was determined to adhere 'according to her conscience' to an apostate Church, an anti-Christian dogma, and a destructive policy for her country, he enunciated a great truth: 'Conscience, Madam, requires light'. If she had gone against her conscience in accepting the Truth she would not have sinned;

but her sin consisted in her refusal to bring her thoughts and conscience into harmony with the will of God as revealed. Which means, in the words of our Lord, that unless the light which is in us apprehends and recognises the higher and truer light of God in His Word, it degenerates into unrelieved darkness. To say, therefore, that sin consists merely of a breach of the 'broken light' which flickers in fallen man is very wide of the mark.

4. Spinoza

The so-called metaphysical view of sin, embedded in several systems of modern philosophy, varies from the crude pantheism of Spinoza to the idealism of Hegel and the unfounded optimism of the Evolutionary hypothesis. When Spinoza came forward with his concept that 'God is all and in all' he meant that God is nothing more than the totality of a complex universe. By this view God has no existence apart from 'the things that are'. The material universe in all its content, and the world of thought, are but His attributes in extension. The whole emphasis here is placed on the immanence of God. As man in his mental processes and physical identity is but a drop in the ocean of infinite Being, it follows that he is destitute of independent personality and permanent existence. In the matter of destiny all that awaits him is absorption into the ever-flowing ocean of Being. There his personal existence comes to an end, just as there is an end to the raindrop when it falls into the sea. As part of God, man is of course morally unaccountable. To him, therefore, there is no such thing as sin; for that would imply an adverse act on the part of one person against another. As God is all, there is no room in the universe for moral or spiritual opposition to Him.

Needless to say this intense pantheism not only does violence to the witness of Revelation with regard to the Being and Personality of God, but to the human consciousness as well. God is immanent in the world, without opposition or 'contradiction', and 'His centre is everywhere'. But God is infinitely more. He is far above every name that can be named. A merely immanent God is as meaningless as a coin having only one side. It is on the doctrine of the everlasting transcendence of God that the truth of His Personality, and His eternal superiority to, and independence of, the creation rests. The universe depends for its existence on the will of God, but in no sense is God dependent for His existence on the universe. He was at its cradle when it was born, and He shall stand by its bier when it shall pass away. 'They shall perish; but Thou remainest.'

No theological school, however advanced, could swallow this view *in toto*. The undue emphasis, however, which its metaphysic placed on the idea of 'God here' quietly invaded the domain of Christian belief, and it was not long before the balance which Christian theism always observed between God's transcendence and immanence was rudely disturbed. A new emphasis came to be placed on God's presence with, and life in, all mankind. When a man like Schleiermacher, under the influence of this philosophy, reduced the Christian life to a mere subjective state by which Christ was brought 'down from above', he gave birth to that theology which dwells on 'Christ in me' and 'God in all'.

The real objective, however, of the doctrine which dwelt so much on this theme of God in man was to strike a blow at the Biblical or Christian doctrine of the depravity of man as a fallen being 'without God and without hope'. The Christian Gospel represents man in himself as 'far off' from God, without any communion with Him, and belonging to a hostile kingdom of darkness where God is not in all his thoughts. This view of man as remote from God through sin was repugnant to the sentimental school of preachers who drew their water from the Spinozan well, and who spoke of God as 'the Father of all' Who loves all and dwells in us all.

This thoughtless unscriptural sentimentalism, now so lavishly poured out from our broadcasting studios and pulpits, and forming the substance of a great amount of the religious literature of our time, is responsible for the ignorance of vast multitudes concerning what the Bible really teaches; about God in His unapproachable holiness, about man under condemnation, and about sin as an impassable barrier between God and man unreconciled.

5. Hegel

The doctrine of man and sin evolved under the influence of this speculation differs greatly from the more plausible view propagated by Hegelianism. To Hegel we may trace the idea of God as realising Himself in one harmonious universe. Hegel's formula of 'Yes—No—Nevertheless' means that all things, good and evil, are working towards a final union. The conflictive elements in the universe—the 'No'—are only apparently in opposition, and are necessary to prevent the world lapsing into a state of moral stagnation. The 'No' and the 'Yes', what we mistakenly call good and evil, are joined in this system by a metaphysical bridge or mediator, the 'Nevertheless' which shall effect the final union of all Reality, whatever the struggle in the process. There is really no evil: there only seems to be evil. This apparent opposition, or 'Antithesis', to the Good is not everlasting, as both the Thesis and the Antithesis, the 'No' as well as the 'Yes', are part of the same ultimate, undivided Reality. This is true not only of evil objectively and historically considered but as it exists in the divided consciousness of man himself.

If ever ideas had legs, Hegel's had! This so-called optimism gave birth to the ideas that 'Reality is one', that sin is 'good in the process', and that there is no eternal distinction between good and evil since these are destined, in the very purpose for which the universe exists, to merge in eternal concord.

At the bar of Scripture this view is, of course, unmitigated moral confusion. The Christian consciousness recoils from it. *The Great Divorce* by C. S. Lewis is an able, if somewhat pictorial, refutation of the idea that good and evil, as existing in man and in the abstract, are finally to merge in a harmonious oneness.

For the Christian believer it is enough to say that God in His Word declares that good and evil are eternally and necessarily in conflict. They can never come together except in that awesome struggle between them which can only end in the destruction of the one, and the triumph of the other. If this view possessed even a shadow of truth we should expect the metaphysical mediator—

the 'Nevertheless'—to effect a growing reconciliation between the 'Yes' and the 'No'. The reverse is the case. For example, we find the modern world, about which Hegel was so hopeful, the inevitable scene of moral forces interlocked in deadly conflict. In one generation the world was twice drenched in blood and shrouded in sorrow, and is now facing a future of unimaginable trials. In other words the nearer evil and good approach each other the greater the evidence of their eternal opposition and irreconcilability. The same thing holds true in the moral consciousness of the renewed soul of man. 'Who shall deliver me?' is the cry of the Christian believer sensible of the workings of the 'law of death' within him. The Christian conscience can never be reconciled to sin because sin is eternally opposed to God.

Hegel's view, however, has been responsible for the emergence of such wickedness as political totalitarianism in modern Europe. He found in the idea of a unified State on earth the very image of God—an illustration of the final synthesis. The ideal State is that in which the individual is nothing and the State is all. The man who can eliminate the conflictive elements, or the exercise of private judgment, in the State, and bring them into submission to the 'Yes', thus achieving an 'individual-less State' of hideous uniformity, approximates in himself and in his work the very purpose and image of God. "Such men are a law unto themselves, and are governed by the imperious direction of their own demonic inspirations. They cannot be judged by short-sighted standards of right and wrong. Such leaders, controlling the destinies of nations, are spirit-possessed personalities devoted to one aim. It is possible that such men may treat great and sacred interests inconsiderately; but so mighty a form must trample down many an innocent flower; and crush to pieces many an object in its path."

The world has had a dread demonstration of what this means. It has turned out that 'the Deification of the State means the bestialisation of man'. Since the devil has not yet sucked this bitter orange entirely it will likely bring more trouble upon man. If the shadow of Adolf Hitler, who imbibed those destructive speculations, is no longer seen in the background, others, under other names, are moving forward to take his place, inspired by the same idea. Milton represents Satan as saying, 'Evil, be thou my good'. This is but a twisted version of his first fatal words to man, 'Ye shall be as gods knowing good and evil'— which means knowing good *through* evil! This is the essential content of Hegel's view. This is the way Satan leads man down the steep path of pride where there is a full manifestation of evil, but where good is eternally unknown.

At this point one is bound to say that Historical Calvinism, and not so much its modern Barthian interpretation, is the only bulwark against the proposed destruction of the individual within such hideous ideological systems as have recently tortured the world, and which still cast their grim shadows over it. No other conception shows the same insistence on the rights, dignity, and freedom of the human personality. Calvinism, so much misunderstood and traduced in this age, is not a 'system'. It is nothing more nor less than the methodical arrangement of the content of the Revelation which God gives of Himself in the Bible. Its even greater insistence on the Sovereignty of God, on His righteousness and manifest graciousness, provides a true spiritual foundation for man. The 'politics' of Calvinism are intensely democratic and humane because they are Scriptural. Man as a being under God, and accountable to Him, has certain great personal rights which he would do well to guard and prize. In the higher sphere of destiny and conscience man has the full right to approach God in his own person through Christ, and to exercise his private judgment in every matter affecting his life and spiritual well-being. This is the freedom which God offers to man through His Son. In contrast Roman Catholicism is on its own profession naked totalitarianism which has largely no basis in the teachings of Christ. There are many modern expressions of the evangelical faith which make their own valuable contribution to Christian existence, but we are persuaded that none of these possesses the integrated and comprehensive solidarity of Historical Calvinism to meet the universal atheism, and the destructive ideology, of this age.

6. Deprivation

A similar view of moral evil goes under the name of a 'limitation of being'. On this theory we are circumscribed by the denial of certain powers. In all our contact with our environment and the external world we experience pain and frustration because of our inability to predetermine whether our course of action will lead us into sunshine or shade. We act within a circle of imperfection, limited in our apprehension, because stinted in our personality. Most of the evil in the world is due to this lack of adequate knowledge, experience, and will power. Therefore, evil and pain are the result of imperfection, impotence and finitude. Whether 'the other side of the hill' is a peaceful 'land of Beulah' or a precipitous chasm of destruction we cannot tell, except through a process of almost blind exploration. If we were all-seeing and all-powerful such errors could not arise! Man, of course, is not responsible for this limitation, and his 'sin' may therefore be reduced to moral nonentity or mere deprivation.

Limited being, however, is not an evil; for by a logical necessity all created beings must be limited in their powers. Yet they may be supremely happy in a sphere of life congenial to their nature, and governed by such a higher will of holiness and goodness as shall never offer the least violence to their perfect freedom. This applies to all beings whether natural or supernatural: to the angel before God's throne, or to the reconciled sinner rejoicing in a new hope. Finite being is not an evil, but the invasion of our natures by something which originally did not belong to them, and the ambition to be more than what God meant us to be, are the causes of all our pain and distress. It is also irrational to speak of man escaping evil only when he shall overcome his limitations. The universe, and all that is beyond it, can only receive One Infinite Being. There is no room for another such.

Nor is pain necessarily an evil thing in the life of man. God's love and mercy must often involve His people in 'a great tribulation' as a necessary discipline to separate them from folly and sin. If man fell painlessly into sin, his deliverance from its power and effect is, however, often accompanied by much spiritual suffering. Many diseases painlessly invade the body of man, but their eradication is often a painful experience.

Again, to reduce the idea of sin to a simple deprivation is contrary to the experience of mankind, both high and low. All the phenomena of guilt, remorse, the involuntary condemnation of conscience when we do wrong, the crude but significant efforts of men, however depraved, to appease the God Whom they feel they have offended, and to Whom they must give account: these prove, in a profound way, not that God has kept something from us, but that we have failed to give Him the glory which is His due, and that we have done, and are doing, something unspeakably shameful against His will, love and nature.

7. Moral evolution

The 'ascent of man' was a favourite theme with a certain class of preachers in the past generation. It was a view which drew its inspiration from the evolutionary theory of man as a biologically and morally ascending being. Happily this view is now on the decline. Abler men than Darwin and Spencer have exposed the untenable suppositions underlying the so-called 'laws' which govern this hypothesis. Unfortunately no other view of man has coloured the outlook of our age more than this. If sin, as this view holds, is the mere expression or 'outbreak' of primitive instincts which man inherited from an irrational ancestry, the Evolutionist can never guarantee that he will ever 'shed' these entirely. At best he can only repress them. But repression, they say, is extremely dangerous. The mind may repress these for a time, but it cannot control them always. Indeed one of the worries of the Freudian psychology is that with the occasional and inevitable eruption of these 'instincts' the mind not only does not control them, but passes under their power. A greater worry is that the deeper we search into the subconscious life of man the more we find that he is also in the toils of utter bondage. Yet the advocates of this view do not despair. The two wars which nearly desolated our Continent are spoken of as 'a dark patch' on the way upward! It is unfortunate that we should have to pass through it. This begging of the question simply means that man himself in his worsening conduct is the final refutation of this view. The 'better and better' dream is shattered. Man's utter failure to adjust himself to a higher ethical and moral world proves the depravity of his nature, and that no culture or civilisation can hold him. His feet are not toward the distant hills of perfection. Rather is he sinking slowly in a slough of despond from which only the merciful hand of God can save him.

It is left to such a so-called 'science' as psychoanalysis—a first cousin to the foregoing view—to go a step beyond and beneath these views, in its treatment of evil as part and parcel of our personalities. Sin is but another name for our repressions, inhibitions and complexes. Every vice is, by this new school, given a scientific name and dress. The final cure for the most shameful tendencies in our fallen nature is to give them reasonable though not full expression. Shame for what we are and what we do is represented as a legacy from a Puritan or Victorian convention. It is only too obvious that the teaching of this 'new outlook' is bearing bitter fruit, for shamelessness is an ominous feature in much of our present day conduct. Let us, however, make no mistake: when we lose a 'sense of shame' all morality goes with it.

8. Moral determinism

The insistence on the part of a large number of modern writers, including our social reformers, that evil is but the product of heredity and environment has commanded much support and sympathy. By this view man is bound as in a prison by his inherited tendencies and environmental influences. These determine both his character and conduct. He has no choice in the matter: he is born, and destined to live, in a persistent groove. He cannot rise upward, though he may well sink below the level which these influences seem to allow! Such determinism is open to several objections. For one thing it strikes at the root of all morality, by throwing the blame of man's conduct on factors external to and beyond himself. It throws overboard such terms as 'ought', 'obligation', and 'responsible to God'. Like other modern theories it fails to explain guilt, conscience and moral choice. The most serious objection to it, however, is that it is a contradiction of experience in two opposite directions. It fails to explain how men and nations have actually risen, through a new impulse from without, from these fixed grooves into a new and wholesome world of moral power and spiritual freedom. There are innumerable instances of men who escaped the power of both heredity and environment, and who created for themselves and others new and happy spheres of existence. Undoubtedly they were given the power to do this by Another; but the fact that God can and does translate men from a state of bondage into freedom is the death blow to this view. A spiritually converted man is God's answer to this philosophy of despair. The man who sings from a joyous experience of God's salvation,

> He took me from a miry pit
> And from the miry clay,
> And on a rock he set my feet
> Establishing my way

is 'closer to Reality' than the philosopher who, unaware of the spiritual world from which Salvation comes to men, weaves his theories from the human situation as it confronts him on his own level.

When Professor William James found in New York converted criminals living normally happy lives he was amazed to find that the change was radical. Personality was cleansed and renewed at its very depths. These men felt themselves in harmony with the universe because they were reconciled to their God. Nothing could explain it but the grace of God.

Man may not only rise upward, but may sink far below his normal environment. Have we not seen with our eyes in recent years how men and nations have jumped the ethical lines on which they had moved for centuries? They jumped these only to plunge into depths of sheer demonism and misery. How a cultured German would have smiled incredulously if in 1934 a prophet had told him that within ten years he and his nation would have sunk to horrible levels of brutality and violence. He would have said with another, 'Is thy servant a dog that he should do such a thing?' And yet he did it.

9. Egoistic hedonism

To many modern people all sin seems to consist in simple selfishness. The end which we ought to set before ourselves is to enhance the happiness and comfort of one another. Let us be kind, and instead of taking let us give. This is indeed a pretty sentiment. Unfortunately the very essence of this hedonistic principle is alive today, on a scale beyond our wildest dreams. This is what man, often an unconscious hypocrite, always preaches but never practises. For example, Germany waged war that it might have *Lebensraum* at the expense of enslaving and displacing millions of human beings. Russia, not satisfied with a whole continent, is seeking to gather a number of smaller nations within its gigantic red orbit. What these and others cannot get by fair means they seek to get by foul. This alone, says the modern man, is sin. Here indeed truth and error are mixed. The chief end of man, however, is not to live in pleasure or even to respect the rights of his fellows, but to glorify his God. Love to God and the fulfilment of our higher duties in relation to Him come before our obligations to men. 'This is the first and great commandment.' It is through the fulfilment of this first duty, whatever pain it may involve, that man ceases to be selfish. Selfishness is a great evil, but evil is more than selfishness. It may well happen also that what many would call selfishness may really be a noble virtue in disguise, and practised for higher ends. The writer remembers over-hearing a lady who worked herself into a state of indignation at the 'selfishness' of the good people of the Isle of Skye who would not facilitate her journey over to that beautiful Isle on the Lord's Day! To her it was a most unchristian and uncharitable act.

What the world needs to-day are men in that sense 'selfish' enough, and strong enough as Christians, to rule over us in the fear of God, and to deprive us, in our physical and moral interests, of such fundamentally selfish 'pleasures' as gambling, degenerate broadcasts, and alcohol abuse. This conception of sin, therefore, works both ways, according to the moral outlook of each man. Was the Lord unreasonable (selfish) when He would not give the people the flesh they lusted after in the desert; or was not the 'selfishness' entirely on their side who wanted their own way and not His?

10. Moral decline

Let us for a moment turn from mere theories to something more portentous. Nearly half a century ago a popular scientist said that "Modern man was not worrying about his sin". This doubtful compliment was exceedingly well received. The statement, however, was a confession of modern man's moral decline and fall. If this has happened it is not because man has advanced beyond the level of conscience or commandment, but because he may have reached a state of something like moral coma—the last symptom of approaching moral death. The most damaging thing about sin is that it hardens the heart, and blinds the eye, to the eternal distinction between good and evil. Sin insentiates the soul, rendering it incapable of seeing that there is something to worry about. If the consciousness of sin is lost in man he is doomed. A sense of 'the evil of sin' in the soul, however feeble, is its last wall of moral resistance. Where the human consciousness is healthy and sane it observes the balance of its own dimensions. It remembers the past, realises the present and anticipates the future. A mere animal 'no tomorrow hath, nor yesterday', as Shakespeare puts it. The glory of man is that as a moral being he both remembers the wrongs of yesterday and is guilty of them in his present experience; and that sense of guilt, he feels, has to do with a future day of reckoning— somewhere. When men care nothing for yesterday or to-morrow in this sense, it means that they have suffered moral disaster. Adolf Hitler once confessed that one of his aims was to eliminate from the human consciousness such 'Jewish and Christian' ideas as conscience or remorse, the fear of God, and the absurd distinction between good and evil.

The solemn fact is that at the end of the War there were men before our judges who had committed the most appalling crimes in history, and on the greatest possible scale, who could not 'take in' that they were guilty of any wrong. They stood in the dock in a condition of moral death—unashamed of what they did, and unaware of what they were.

It is exactly this loss of moral sense and moral responsibility on the part of man that places our world in its greatest danger, and prepares it for its greatest catastrophe.

Chapter III

Why evil?

THE DEEP

All the views which we attempted to state in the previous Chapter have one thing in common: they fail to bring full conviction to the mind. When all is said we instinctively feel that there is 'something else'. The fact is that beyond the horizon of human observation and thought lies the great deep from which evil has its source. Beyond the data which the conduct of humanity and the conjectures of philosophy provide the questions inevitably arise, 'From whence?' and 'What is it?' The Biblical account of human creation, as we have observed already, is that man came upon the scene a perfect moral being— 'without sin'. It also informs us that evil invaded the world from without. An assault, in other words, was made on this planet by preternatural 'principalities and powers'. This is a fact of Revelation apart from which we can never understand what evil really is.

The tragedy behind our contemporary and historical world is exactly this—the failure or unwillingness to recognise the preternatural origin of sin. We see an ever-recurring disintegration and collapse of our painfully built 'worlds', and the ever-recurring attempt to heal the wound by our own ever-frustrated efforts. We are unwilling to believe that the restlessness and disasters which make up our days on earth have a permanent supernatural background, and that to escape these evils, we must betake ourselves to the great and ever-available supernatural salvation provided in 'the everlasting Gospel'. How easy it is to apprehend the good world of what ought to be; but like the desert mirage the fair vision never becomes a reality. The mirage never becomes the placid pool which we hope for. Our ideals never become certainties. Why? Because when God shows us the way to health and deliverance we insist either on staying here as we are, or on walking in the opposite direction. This is man's supreme folly, in the presence of which God Himself exclaims, 'O that they were wise, and considered their latter end'.

In discussing in this Chapter 'how evil came to be', no effort is made at being wise above what God has revealed in His infallible Word, or to understand what lies behind the curtain which hides forever from our view 'the depths of Satan' or the 'How' and 'Why' of evil in its beginnings in another world than ours.

We can say, however, that moral and spiritual corruption begins whenever the creature separates from God. 'Abide in Me' is the law of eternal life. Just as this planet would perish if it left its orbit and wandered away from its solar path and influence, so angels or men, the moment they forsake God, the Fountain of Life and Light, immediately become subject to corruption. That corruption can never be arrested unless the creature, in the sovereign goodness and mercy of God, is brought back to its original favour, and in that favour established.

The deliberate forsaking of God, and the attempt to live in independence of Him, mean moral and spiritual death. Did those angels then 'who kept not their first estate' aspire to 'live their life in their own way'? Did they say in effect, and in the words of a modern writer, 'This is our business, not yours; we will stand in our own rights'? Did they aspire to be nouns and not adjectives? This ambition to occupy a corner of the universe where they could exercise their own authority and enjoy the privilege of 'Home Rule' seems to have been one of the fatal poison drops in the minds of those fallen beings.

This pride of life, this ambition to be first and not second, is certainly a fundamental characteristic of all evil. It obviously had its birth when Satan began—as he must have done—to admire his own glory and power as if these were essential to himself, and not derived from the God on Whose goodness he was so wholly dependent, and Who had clothed him in those shining garments of life and immortality. This shifting of the eye from the One Who alone is worthy of praise, to arrogate to himself the independence and worship which belong to God alone, constitutes the very essence of evil.

That Satan aspired to deity—that is, to be the object of worship—may be understood from the demands he made on the Eternal Son of God Himself. 'All these will I give Thee, if Thou wilt fall down and worship me.' Here, then, we have an insight into the heart of the devil, the father of the first lie. In this demand the attempt was made to dethrone and debase God Himself in the Person of the Divine Son. Finding on earth, in the form of a Man, and veiled in the garments of humiliation, the One Whom he refused to worship in Heaven, he sought by the most subtle temptation ever devised to subordinate His changeless will to his own. There is therefore deep truth in Milton's words.

> His pride had cast him out of Heaven with all his host
> Of rebel angels; by whose aid aspiring
> To set himself in glory above his peers,
> He trusted to have equalled the most High.

Biblical Revelation provides us with another clue which might help us to understand the 'Why?' of evil. It has to do with the government of the world by the Messiah. Him has God the Father made both King and Lord over all. By the decree of God the Father He is 'Heir of all things'. Not only so, but all power and authority in Heaven and on earth are His. Into His ever-prospering hand are committed the immutable redemptive and providential purposes of the Eternal. This glory given to Christ none can share. The universe is part of His dominions both by right of Creation and by right of gift. 'The Father loveth the Son, and hath given all things into His hand.' His all-embracing and exclusive rule makes Him the First and the Last, the Alpha and the Omega. Which means that the universe in its beginning, continuity and consummation (as well as in the whole of its alphabetic or manifold content) consists in, and belongs to, Christ. Every creature among angels and men is put in dependence on and in subordination to Him.

The idea is often expressed in the massive theology of the Puritan age that the declaration of this truth, and the manifestation of this Person Who was from everlasting in the bosom of the Father, were what first evoked Satan's opposition. The 'truth' that Christ is Lord over all, and the only Redeemer and Messiah appointed by the ordinance of Heaven, was the truth in which Satan refused to abide. This marked the first dread opposition to God's will. Therefore, he is the father, or origin, of the lie. Evil began there: in saying 'No' to God. It was exactly this truth which the Jews opposed when they sought to destroy Christ. In their opposition Christ detected an exact resemblance to 'the lie' perpetrated in another world. And this was why He faced them with the words, "Ye are of your father the devil, and the lusts of your father ye will do. He was a murderer from the beginning, and abode not in the truth, because there is no truth in him." Their refusal to recognise the truth of His Messiahship pointed to their alliance with the 'Prince of this world'.

It is a fact of Revelation also that from all eternity, when all future creation came within the scope of divine omniscience, God and Christ took a particular delight in a certain Place and People. 'God so loved the world'. . .'Christ also loved the Church'. Christ then rejoiced in the prospect of an inhabited world, and in the prospect of coming into this world, not in the nature of angels, but in the nature of man. He would honour men more than angels, not only by assuming man's nature, but by bringing this new and complex being into a higher and more honourable relationship to Himself than angels can ever enjoy.

The Church in all its members is 'the King's daughter' in relation to the Father; 'the Lamb's wife' in her covenant relation to the Son. This is her high honour. 'Since thou wast precious in My sight, thou hast been honourable, and I have loved thee.' Angels are 'all ministering spirits sent forth to minister for them who shall be heirs of salvation'.

Did Satan then resent being left out from having any share in the government of this world? Did he resent the all-embracing rule of the Messiah, and his own everlasting subordination to Him? Did he oppose the greater honour conferred on the inferior creation of men than on himself? Did he refuse to bow his head at the manifestation of the Eternal and Personal Word Who dwelt in the inner light of Jehovah's bosom—a light to which no finite creature can approach? When God said, 'Let all the angels of God worship Him' did he and those who followed him in his rebellion say 'No?' These are solemn questions which we merely ask but which arise from what appears in the several rays of light thrown on this solemn and mysterious subject by God Himself in His inerrant Word. Beyond that we dare not go. Evil is known here only 'in part'. In the words of Dr Daniel Lamont, it is a thing so terrible that reason could not stand a full view of it. Only in eternity will those who forsake God know what it really is.

How could evil happen? How moral perfection, even within finite personalities, could degenerate into absolute and incurable wickedness, is a question too deep and mysterious for man to answer. How could this happen by a spontaneous act of the will, without coercion, influence or temptation from without? How could a glorious angel, joyous in its freedom and service in God's Presence, become a devil? No man can tell. The Platonic idea that no reasonable creature would voluntarily leave a state of perfection and happiness for a different way of life is contradicted by the Fall of angels and men. To say that they did this from the motive of rising higher than they were does not alter the fact that perfect, though limited beings, left to the freedom of their own will, may and did fall to the lowest hell.

When Christ created this world, and prepared it as the temporary dwelling-place for man, He inaugurated a new kingdom. Adam was the son of God, inasmuch as God created him in His image, for His glory, and over whom He was to rule in love. This kingdom Satan opposed, and sought to reign within it himself. In proof of this we have the devil present in the world at its very beginning, as Christ's rival and as the world's professed Prince of Power. His kingdom he set up in opposition to the kingdom of God's dear Son. In the Garden, which God prepared, Satan found two beings who bore every sign of God's workmanship and love. And deceptively coiled at the base of the forbidden Tree, incarnate wickedness uttered a word which opened the door of infinite sorrow for man. 'Hath God said? Nay. . .' To man's acting on the suggestions of that lying voice we trace the entrance of pain, death and destruction into the world of time and into eternity itself. This it was that sent a pang and a groan through the whole creation, and which caused the ever-blessed God to weep and groan in His Spirit as He stood in our nature before the fact of death. Because man listened to that voice he stands before God, as Adam did, helpless and hopeless in himself, and shivering in his ever-increasing guilt.

Chapter IV

The origin of sin

THE DARK INVADING FLOOD

The several problems related to the introduction of evil into this world in the very morning of man's life cannot be discussed here. The Augustinian saying that God would destroy evil if He could, or could destroy it if He would, is supposed to raise logical difficulties reflecting on the power and goodness of God. Such arguments, however unanswerable in their logical form, are fundamentally presumptuous. It is a mysterious fact that God in harmony with His unchangeable decree and in the unsearchable wisdom of His holy Providence permitted evil to cross the threshold of his once superlative world. This He did without approving of it, while in His infinite holiness He is also eternally unrelated to its origin and works. The Author of conscience and of the Moral Law is essentially good, and can do nothing but good. The Rock of Israel can do no iniquity. A deep 'woe' rests on those who strive with their Maker— charging Him either with having mismanaged the government of the world, or with showing any reluctance to save man from self-destruction.

God created a perfect world and a perfect man; but man with open eyes devised the instrument of his own death and dug his own grave. The man whom God created to rule the world according to His good and perfect will put himself under the government of 'the lawless one', whose aim was to bring chaos and disorder into the world through the corruption of man's nature. The more therefore in our present plight we endeavour to rule the world in our own way, and not according to the Divine law which promises 'great peace' to those who love it, the deeper we sink into physical misery and moral lawlessness.

When evil did challenge the rule of the Most High, in His own world His goodness is proved by the fact that immediately after his Fall He initiated for man a redemptive process of salvation and recovery. This process is threefold.

(a) He decreed that all evil should be overruled to the good of His people in this world, and finally overcome by His Eternal Son in His redeeming act on the Cross of Calvary.
(b) He made the entrance of evil into the world the occasion for the manifestation of His power and glory. God, in fact, brings all His attributes on to the stage of human history both in the salvation of His people, and in the destruction of their foes. He will show His power in each of these. History, as it works toward this irresistible end, is really 'His Story'.
(c) Man immediately after his Fall was informed of God's redeeming purpose. He was given a glimpse through the vista of prophetic time of 'the way of escape' through 'the Seed of the woman'. He was given more. God, we believe, blessed him with the gift of faith which put him in instant possession of a new hope and of eternal deliverance through the coming One.

To relegate the doctrine of the Fall itself into the category of theological myth is to disbelieve God, deny the meaning of history, and misunderstand man in his present plight.

God affirms that the Fall really happened. This is the testimony of Scripture and the precursor and implication of Revelation itself. The entrance of sin into the world is the occasion of the self-revealing of a gracious and just God. To disbelieve the doctrine of the Fall of man is to deny that God has spoken to this world either in His written or Personal Word; in other words the Bible and Christ are destitute of all supernatural meaning. To disbelieve this, however, is to stumble on the firm rock of prophetic truth in its manifold and accurate fulfilment; on the Rock of Christ's Deity and Incarnation, evidenced in His sinless life; in His works which none but God could do; and in

His resurrection by which He proved to be the very 'Son of God with power'.

Man himself, however, is a perpetual witness to the Fall both in his consciousness and conduct. He knows, and often acutely feels, that he is far removed from what he ought to be. This proves that he was once what he is not now. If man had evolved from irrational and non-moral forms of life he should have no consciousness of moral *lapsus*. His admission that he ought to be what he is not is a final refutation of the metaphysical and evolutionary hypotheses, as this 'regret', however vague, has to do with a sense of loss of a better status and condition, and not with a dimly apprehended and ideal future.

This dim sense of loss expresses itself in a thousand ways. Man does 'many things' in the hope of finding the 'one thing'. And while the body, and to some extent the mind, find their gratification 'in nature', there is in the depths of human consciousness the deep persistent sense of deprivation which is nothing less than the loss of the presence and communion of God. Man's bereaved and widowed nature, with its sorrow and restlessness, goes back to the hour when he stood in his guilt and loneliness 'among the trees of the garden' with his back to God. Man is the only 'animal' who is dissatisfied with mere 'things', or with mere nature. Sheep and cattle which eat grass—though made subject to vanity and affected by our sin—rest contentedly on the summer meadow. The crane and the swallow satisfy their instincts and nature when they mate, migrate, and build their nests. They were made for nature, but man's soul was made to receive an infinitely higher Good—God Himself in possession. This persistent sense of loss through sin is the secret of man's plight and spiritual poverty.

Human conduct is an even a greater proof of the Fall than the disturbed human consciousness. In his outward behaviour man is a restless being, fumbling in the dark in search of the needed but unknown good. Each new 'god' whose altar he erects finds him still unsatisfied; and the altar which he erects 'to the Unknown God' is the symbol of both his disillusionment and his tragedy. Man has in fact turned the world into one gigantic Vanity Fair in the vain hope of finding happiness in broken cisterns instead of in the Fountain of living waters.

Written history may not be wholly accurate; but the substance of what we know may be summed up in one verse of Scripture. "So I returned and considered all the oppressions that are done under the sun; and behold the tears of such as were oppressed, and they had no comforter; and on the side of the oppressors there was power, but they had no comforter."

Need we go to history or antiquity to find a convincing proof of man's Fall? As he stands at this moment in this so-called modern world, is he not, in the most obvious sense of the word, helpless and fallen? As Adam blamed the woman, he may in his pride blame other factors and persons for his terrible predicament and receding prospects; but in his heart of hearts he knows that the cause of his plight is in his own sinful breast, and in his wrong relationship to God.

In *The Problem of Pain* C. S. Lewis states that whatever man's first sin was it must have been inconceivably great before such dire results both in time and beyond time follow in its path. To look upon the sin of Adam and Eve as a trifling breach of the Divine command, which God might have charitably winked at, is to fail to appreciate the great moral issues involved in their crime.

Those who admit that the Fall took place, but who say that the punishment meted out to man is out of all proportion to the crime, must be confronted with the light which God in His Word throws on this very objection. Only then do we see that God is just in the sentence pronounced.

Man's sin was against the light of knowledge. God took every care to show him that his chief glory, as a rational being, consisted in obedience to a higher will than his own. In the words of Pascal, obedience to God is the highest privilege of a reasonable being. To quote Dr Daniel Lamont, 'It is for God to command, and for man to obey'.

The visible symbol of God's will for man was a lovely tree in a fruitful garden, while his perfect freedom consisted in his access to the fruit of every other tree, and in his rule over the rest of the creatures. Man, therefore, was created free in the highest sense; for obedience to Divine law is the highest expression of true freedom. When man trespassed by appropriating what was not his, his sin did not consist 'in the eating of one apple' but in repudiating God's will as it was objectively symbolized before his very eye, and by extinguishing the full light of his own spirit which God had blessed with knowledge. Man's sin was not therefore an experiment the result of which he could not foresee. 'In the day that thou eatest thereof thou shalt surely die.' Neither the Bible nor the Christian conscience argues that this sentence was unjust or arbitrarily pronounced.

All sin whether committed by the first man or by us now is exceedingly sinful since it is committed against the very Being of God, and in His sight. We stand before Him as we are, 'without the mask' and laden with the sins of yesterday, to-day and to-morrow. 'Thou hast set our iniquities before Thee; our secret sins in the light of Thy countenance.' This is why we should ever be ashamed of sin. It is committed in the full view of Eternal Holiness. This is why, in the words of the late Professor Bowman, some have stood before God in the crisis of their discovered guilt ashamed not only of what they had done, but ashamed of existing at all.

The modern objection that the sin of Adam and Eve has little significance for man now, cannot be got over by merely denying the federal theology of Calvinism. The first man was a representative person, in whose Fall we are all involved and in whom we suffered judicial condemnation. In fact the sinfulness of the race cannot be Scripturally grounded in any other consideration than in this federal solidarity. The Covenant which God made with Adam embraced all his posterity, so that 'all mankind, descending from him, by ordinary generation, sinned in him, and fell with him in his first transgression'. It is therefore true that the relationship between him and us is that between the fountain and its stream. The unanimous testimony of Scripture is that because of one man's disobedience death passed over the race whose covenant head he was, and that the ordinary stream of humanity descending from him is subject to physical, spiritual and eternal death.

Death then is the result of the Fall. Those who deny the doctrine of the Fall reject the idea that there is any causal connection between physical death and sin. No doubt death reigned in the organic, irrational world before man was created.

Death is a law which necessarily operates in the organic world. Man, however, stands in a different category to 'the beasts which perish'. He was made 'in God's image'. God also made him a living soul when He breathed into his nostrils 'the breath of life'. This conferred upon man the great gift of immortality. He cannot 'cease to be' even when he suffers physical dissolution or spiritual death. In his sinless state there was an ever-flowing stream of life communicated to his soul and body by unbroken communion with his Maker. If matter has a spiritual co-efficient which makes it capable of perpetual co-operation with the spirit, man's physical nature would not have perished had he retained his communion with the Fountain of life. 'Death came upon all through sin. . .'

And when the Bible speaks of death through sin, it does not mean merely the separation of soul and body, but the separation of both from God. The bodily death of a Christian is not death, for Christ said, 'If a man believe in Me, though he were dead yet shall he live, and I shall raise him up at the last day'.

Sin is not only a loss of life, but a loss of status. The banishment of the spirit from the presence of God, in a state of alienation and corruption, is an immeasurable Fall. The return of the body to 'destruction' followed this downfall of the spirit into its bondage of the grave of trespass and sin.

Modern religious thought, while far from accepting this view of the Fall of man, still admits that something is far wrong with man. Man is often represented as more than half a fool who just will not live up to his 'better self'. He is 'sick', but not 'unto death'. There is still a wholesome stratum of moral health embedded somewhere in the hidden depths of his being. If only he gave himself a chance, or gave God a chance, to cultivate this 'better self' he might be fairly led towards the uplands of peace and health. Although the Bible, and indeed, the history of man, make it clear that sin is an ever-worsening disease, a species of theological Couéism [i.e., psychotherapy by autosuggestion:-Ed.] still persists even within the community of Churches. In fact, the whole approach of 'the modern pulpit' to man is based on this supposition, that man has a large measure of goodwill, grace and spiritual health, which he should cultivate for the good of his neighbour and himself. This is the persistent illusion of an anaemic humanism which lies far remote from the Christian view of man as a fallen sinner before God.

Not long ago the writer read a book by a professed evangelical minister who offered a criticism of the great Welsh Revival. The book was written in the early years of this century. The writer ended his book by suggesting, in a kindly mood of great goodwill, that as human nature was becoming nicer and better, and man himself sweeter and kinder, revivals might be considered as 'things of the past'. They were but the emotional crises of man in his upward climb. The book was written in a time of material prosperity, and in a land of peace. Our poets then sang that because God was in His heaven all was right with the world. Unfortunately, the book survived long enough to be read in 1942; and a very unfair reader, who had spent days and nights in one of our bombed cities, amid blood and tears, wrote the words 'Heil Hitler' on the margin opposite the 'sweeter and kinder' sentence.

We have really to do with God's judgment on man, and not man's judgment on himself. God Himself declares that the deeper He searches into the very thoughts and purposes of man the more ill-favoured his condition becomes.

In the clear light of the Divine Law man can show God nothing but his sin. The relation, in fact, between man and his Maker is that of a proven criminal to a just Judge, or that of a defiled being in the presence of unsullied purity.

Chapter V

Redemption

THE BIRTH OF A NEW DAY

The redemption of man is the eternal witness to God's love, wisdom, and power. It is the unfathomable miracle of mercy working opposite man's ill-deserving. The most solemn moment in the history of mankind was when the first man stood before God to hear of that grace which would restore him to God and secure blessedness. It marked the birth of a new day and a new hope for a being whose sin left him without God and without hope in the world. The facts which one should stress with regard to the doctrine of Redemption could be stated in the following order.

1. Christ is Redeemer

Since evil is a preternatural power this Redemption is also necessarily supernatural, and is wrought out in a supernatural Person. The Person who redeems us must stand equal to God both in power and glory. He must have all the qualities and the attributes of Deity. In other words, He must be the true God Himself. But for the redemption of man He must be more. He must have the true nature of man free from all its sin. The dishonour done to the Name and the will of God by man's disobedience was so great that He could never accept atonement for sin from any person inferior to Himself. Nor would he accept atonement from a person who was not in a real sense a man.

It was man who came short of God's glory, and therefore man must pay what he owes to God in His law under which man was placed, and in His justice by which man was held. In the matter of our redemption this was the deep necessity behind the Incarnation, or 'the mystery of Godliness'—God appearing in the world in the Person of the eternal Son and 'in the *likeness* of sinful flesh' [author's italics]. He came not in the likeness of man before the Fall, but in his likeness after all the sorrow and griefs of sin had cast their heavy shadows over his soul and body. He took our nature, that in that very nature He might redeem ours, and make us partakers of His own. He bore our image that we might in the perfection of eternity bear His. The nature of man which He united to His Divine Person constituted a perfect manhood. In that nature He wrought out the righteousness which the unrelenting rectitude of the Law of God still required of man, but which man could never give. It is when God covers us in this righteousness as with a robe that we stand before Him uncondemned. 'For Christ is the end of the Law for righteousness to every one that believeth.' By this righteousness imputed to man by sovereign love, and received by the faith which God gives, he is no longer a criminal at the bar of Divine justice, but a son in good standing in the household of God.

2. The Holy Spirit frees the Redeemed from the dominion of sin

Evil also is a power of such inconceivable greatness that only God, in the whole range of His omnipotence, could overcome and destroy. For this end then was the Son of God manifested, that He might destroy the works of the devil. The devil had the power of death in this world, and in the soul of man, and into this world the Mighty One came to vanquish him in his own dominions. He triumphed over him openly on His Cross. The death of Christ was 'the death of death', the end of sin, and the judgment of this world and its prince.

This inconceivable power of evil is the stupendous fact which both Christ Himself and the Church recognised. "And I looked and there was none to help; and I wondered that there was none to uphold: therefore Mine own arm brought salvation to Me; and My fury it upheld Me."

The prayer of the Church was exactly this desire and longing for the manifestation of her Almighty Lord as the promised

Deliverer. "Gird Thy sword upon Thy thigh, O most mighty. . . and Thy right hand shall teach Thee terrible things."

In this connection the Bible also recognises what the Christian in his experience knows: that even within the redeemed soul of man, evil, though broken in its dominion, has such power —and is so much in possession—that it requires God in the Person of the Spirit, in a ministry of life and grace, to deliver us from its indwelling power. The Holy Spirit, for this very reason, is the most precious Gift which Christ obtained for men by His death and exaltation. Redemption, therefore, both in its objective and subjective completeness and glory, is the work of God.

It is by this redemption that sin is put away 'as far as east is distant from the west'. It rests wholly on the merits of Christ as God's Son, and on the absolute perfection of

His finished work. It was exactly this knowledge of being delivered from condemnation by faith in Christ and His obedience that enabled Paul to 'thank God' at the very moment when he was acutely conscious of sin dwelling in him. He rejoiced in the knowledge that as Christ died for him, and as his justification by faith in Christ was therefore absolute and eternal, so also his entire deliverance from 'the sinful law' working in his members was only a matter of time.

3. Redemption frees us from ignorance of God

Redemption delivers the soul from the evil of ignorance of God. In his first epistle to the Corinthians Paul proves that the world by its wisdom (or philosophy) knew not God, and that the highest expression of that wisdom had actually given a concrete symbol of its utter ignorance of the only Living and True God. It had failed utterly to apprehend final Reality. 'To the Unknown God' was the altar erected on Mars Hill by the pupils of Plato, and it is an altar which an agnostic such as Bertrand Russell might erect today in his English garden!

God is known only in the face of Jesus Christ, and there can be no apprehension of His glory, as there can be no admission into His Presence, but through His mediation and by the precious blood of His Cross.

What lies within the veil, and beyond all human perception, shall ever remain a mystery to those who prefer the rushlight of their own reason to the clear light which streams from the Cross of Christ. It is here that millions whose eyes God has opened have known Him in His power, wisdom and grace. It is here that God in His reconciling love discloses Himself to those who unlearn their own 'way of thinking' and who are made new-born babes in His school.

4. Redemption puts Christ's obedience down to our account

Freedom from all legal bondage is the immediate blessedness of redeemed men. All man-made 'religions' have one thing in common: they attempt by a multiplicity of self-prescribed and self-imposed duties, penances, and tortures to attain to righteousness and to purchase the favour of God—or of the gods. Christ found this even in the Jewish Church of old, which had declined so far from the faith of Abraham. It was this which brought Him to say, in infinite pity, 'Come unto Me, all ye that labour and are heavy laden, and I will give you rest'. He found men in bondage to a law of carnal commandments. They were ever striving, but never arriving. This, in fact, is what is found in the Roman, Greek, Anglican and other Churches of to-day. Christ fulfilled 'all righteousness' in relation to the ceremonial law with its tedious and never-ending ritual. The Church therefore is no longer a child under tutors and governors in the nursery with its toys, candles, and pinafores, and groaning to be free. It has come of age; it has 'put away childish things'. Its worship and life now lie in the higher realm of the Spirit according to the truth of the Gospel.

The same thing is true of all believers in their relation to the eternal Moral Law. We are not justified by the deeds of this Law. Its great demands are infinitely beyond the power of fallen man to fulfil. Paul utterly despaired of himself as he stood before its towering and unscalable heights. 'The Law is holy, just and good, but I am carnal and sold under sin.' Therefore Christ redeemed us from its curse as a covenant broken in our hands, by fulfilling all its requirements and suffering all its penalty for us. True, the Law of God is the supreme rule of conduct for all Christians, but its fulfilment can never be the condition of salvation because none but the Son of God ever climbed, or ever shall climb, this great height in his own merits and power. The glory of redemption consists in this very fact. Christ's perfect obedience to, and honouring of, the Law, when we receive Him as our Righteousness, is put down to our account, as if we had done this impossible thing ourselves. If this is not grace for poor man, what is?

5. Redemption depends on God's unchangeableness

The Christian Gospel also provides for 'the final perseverance' and triumph of all who are saved. The first Adam lost both himself and us. He was only a mere creature subject to change. The second Adam is an unchangeable Person Whose people are kept by the power of God through faith unto salvation. The life which He gives is eternal. 'I give unto them eternal life, and they shall never perish, neither shall any man pluck them out of My hand.' The redeemed soul is embraced within the whole redeeming purpose of God, the end of which is as certain as its beginning. 'Whom He foreknew. . . them He also glorified.' The symbol of God's everlasting covenant with the Church is not the bow in an evanescent cloud, but an unfading rainbow 'like unto an emerald' about the Throne on which Christ sits in the cloudless Heaven above.

It is therefore the unchangeableness of God, in the covenant of grace (and not our poor faltering steps) which is the foundation of all Christian security and consolation. It was this that brought comfort to believers in every age. "Lift up your eyes to the heavens and to the earth beneath; for the heavens shall vanish away like smoke, and the earth shall wax old like a garment. . . but My salvation shall be forever, and My righteousness shall not be abolished."

6. Redemption depends on a risen Christ

Moreover an efficient redemption requires the evidence that the Lord of Glory did actually overcome, and that although He died, He now lives to bestow that which by His death He procured, and to bring the subjects of His mercy to that place where He is Himself. The Christian has a two-fold evidence that Christ is risen from the dead: the unassailable evidence furnished by the Gospels, and the witness which he has in himself as risen with Christ. Christian conversion means a rising with Christ, the newborn life in communion with the ever-living Lord in Heaven. To tell a Christian that his personal redemption and regeneration, and his daily communion with his Lord, are mere illusions is to deny Reality in its nearest approach to man. 'We know. . .and believe. . .and are sure. . .that this is the True God and eternal life.' There is no such absolute certainty about any other world of experience.

7. Redemption brings Christ's consolation to those who preach the Gospel

By His death, resurrection and exaltation Christ furnished the Church with the message and power necessary for the salvation of man. On the eve of His passing into the Heavens He commissioned His apostles to 'go into all the world and preach the Gospel to every creature'. They were to be heralds of the one theme: that Christ died to redeem us, and that He rose again for our justification. The Apostolic Church never deviated from these glorious truths. Its message, however, was not a bald reiteration of historical and theological truth, however stupendous that truth was in itself. It was a message energised by the Holy Ghost. The Word was with power, for the Risen Lord was with them. By the power of the Gospel the Prince of this world was cast out. Evil, at last, had to reckon with weapons more powerful than any it could forge. Its strongholds in heathen hearts and in the pagan world lay shattered before the impact of the New Power. The kingdom of darkness and death was invaded by the Life and the Light of God, and the

Gospel moved on like a river in full flood, and as irresistible as the waves of the sea. The dark malignant soul of paganism pined away in the new atmosphere created by the Gospel. To all its enemies the Church itself became 'terrible as an army with banners'. The Sun of Righteousness had truly risen on the moral deserts of this world with healing in His wings.

'Lo, I am with you always.' How easy it is to repeat this consoling assurance! Let us never forget, however, that this great promise was conditional on the Church preaching the Gospel of Jesus Christ. 'Preach the Gospel, and lo, I am with you.'

That Gospel is for all time enshrined in the full, infallible revelation that we have in all the Scriptures. By any denial or diminution of that Gospel, or by adding the word of man to the Word of God, the Church would imperil its existence and forfeit its very life in the withdrawal of the presence and power of the Lord in her ministry.

Even the primitive Church had to contend with 'gospels' and tendencies which endangered its existence. The Pauline warning, 'Quench not the Spirit. . .Grieve not the Holy Spirit of God' served as a red light to warn the Church of how enfeeblement and disaster might really come.

God's Spirit, in fact, will never accompany any message but the word of reconciliation. Where the blood is not in the vessel; where 'Christ crucified' is not our theme, then no fire will descend from Heaven to witness that God has pleasure in our work. Rather will He hide His face and withhold His power, and leave us to pine away in our miseries and sins with nothing in view 'but a certain fearful looking-for of judgment'.

Chapter VI

The Church in decay

THE LONG VOYAGE INTO THE LAND OF NIGHT

There is a 'far cry' of two thousand years between now and the day when Peter stood arrayed in Pentecostal power on the streets of Jerusalem.

During the intervening centuries the Christian Church, both Apostolic and Reformed, has had its periods of light and shade. There can be no doubt that in these darkening times it has touched astonishing depths of spiritual decline. It looks as if it were 'a spent force' in the world. The initial and irresistible impulse which marked the Pentecostal age is gone; and the new life which revived it at the Reformation is now a mere memory. Many therefore conclude that 'Christianity is played out', and that while the Gospel itself suited a more primitive state of society it is inadequate to solve all the problems created by an advancing science in the spaceless, ideological world of to-day. There are two things, however, that we should bear in mind: the modern representation of Christianity is profoundly wrong; and something of an appalling nature has happened to the visible Church itself. It is with this last point that we are now concerned.

Before the Apostles left the world they saw the first beginnings of what they called 'the mystery of iniquity' working within the Church. They saw the arrival of a spirit of lawless ambition, and a striving on the part of some for 'preeminence'. The great example of Christian humility which our Lord gave as the eternal and essential characteristic of the true Christian ministry began to be opposed. Pride, the eternal characteristic of all evil, sought to displace Christian humility and man's word strove to displace the Word of Christ. The shadow of evil, however, was not then bigger than a man's hand; but the apostles had sufficient discernment to see that the arrival of this spirit aimed at the destruction of the Christian Gospel, as it was delivered in all its primitive purity by Christ and His apostles. It was in fact the return of the spirit which had lodged in the pagan world, seeking, in the guise of God's emissary, to occupy a place in God's House. Those who have traced the 'dark ambitions' lurking behind the beginnings, growth, and maturity of Roman Catholicism have found it to be the whole cult of paganism revived and baptised, and constituting in form, spirit, and aim, the very antithesis of New Testament Christianity. Its inconsistent and deceptive adherence to many Christian doctrines is nullified by its acceptance of pagan practices which have no ground in the Christian Revelation.

The triple crown of pride on the head of 'an enthroned and infallible Pope' is the visible proof that within the Roman Church, at least, all Christian grace and humility have long since withered and died.

In the apocalyptic vision John saw two Churches which were to pass on the stage of historical time: 'Babylon the Great' and the 'New Jerusalem'. On the page of Scripture the one stands for Satan's imitation of the Christian Church—the other for Christ's redeemed and only Bride. It is, moreover, an impossibility to find in history any correspondence to, or fulfilment of, this vision except in the Roman heresy. This fact can never be too frequently stated. Candid Romanists themselves have admitted as much.

The presence of this 'Church' in the modern world is its greatest menace. The writer, and many others, have elsewhere discussed, with a fulness of detail, the direct culpability of the Roman Church by following a policy of sheer and unmoral opportunism in encouraging the Second World War. This is a truth which the Church of Rome, with its magnificent propaganda, has tried hard to conceal and which many Protestants, who look only on the surface, cannot believe.

Now that the shadow of a vicious Communism is over Europe, and challenging Romanism on its own hearth, the Church, conscious of moral and spiritual destitution in the presence of this rising tide, is appealing to the world to 'save Christianity' from the Russian danger. If, however, as Dr Wylie and many other students of Scripture believe, political Communism is to be God's great sword in the destruction of Romanism, we should hesitate to fall in with those who so loudly advocate 'a common Christian front against a common foe'. After all, Romanism has proved itself to be as great an enemy of the Church of Christ as any other anti-Christian system. We should therefore do well, as these spiritual powers clash, to stand still and see the salvation of the Lord.

In 1854 Mr J. C. Philpot of *The Gospel Standard* predicted from a study of the scroll of prophecy that Russia, dominated by a powerful aspiration, would one day sweep over Europe, but that it would finally perish on the mountains of Israel. If the old and corrupt Papal system falls before this cold and awful blast from the North we shall only witness the fulfilment of God's Word and the execution of His judgment. At present the Roman Church is in a state of panic; and the danger to the world lies in the fact that panic is contagious. A few years ago, for example, statements appeared in certain American newspapers urging America to 'finish off' Russia before she has time to arm herself or be able to make use of the atomic bomb. As Dr Joseph MacCabe said before a Glasgow audience, the Church means by this 'holy war' 'a sudden, savage, and treacherous assault on that nation' with this new catastrophic weapon. Between a godless Communism and a corrupt Catholicism we have nothing to choose; but these 'alarms' are beyond doubt taking effect, and should the great world powers clash we should know from whence arose the main provoking influence. When the Church itself glances at the world situation, it can offer no hope or help.

A schoolboy with a few elementary lessons in moral philosophy and diplomacy could write the vague and non-committal exhortations which the Pope delivers from time to time to a frightened, anxious world.

In his book *God and the Atom*, Ronald Knox dwells on the phrase, 'Where do we go from here?' It is the last word in moral bewilderment. His attempt to assess the significance for the future of what happened at Hiroshima is a confession that his Church has no clue in its hand to lead it out of its labyrinthine confusion. It has no ray of light with which to show mankind the path of salvation or even survival. The world tragedy, then, before our eyes to-day is that of a Church luring in its wake, by the siren notes of a deceptive propaganda, nations which have ceased to hear the Word of God but which adapt their policy to the voice of the Vatican.

But what of the Protestant Churches? The rediscovery of the *New Testament* in 1500, and the consequent return to apostolic Christianity, marked the creation of the great community of Reformed Churches. The Bible was once again enthroned in the Church, and Roman dogma and pretension disowned. While the Reformed Church remained in the truth it went on its way renovating and uplifting sinful and weary nations which had groaned under the oppressions of the Papal Church.

The hovering shadow of evil, however, similar to that which troubled the apostolic Church and which culminated in the Roman perversion, rested on the Reformed Church in Europe. There is a fascinating similarity in all the efforts of Satan to corrupt both man and the Church God created for His service, and directed by His Word alone. The spirit which began to trouble the Reformed Church over a century ago attacked the foundation on which the Church is built—the trustworthiness of the Bible. Man placed himself on a throne on which he might sit in judgment on God in His Word. 'Are Biblical claims and history authentic?' was the question which saw the beginning of a work of critical destruction. The Bible in all its august claims to be the inerrant Word of God was looked at through the suspicious eyes of an immature and unclarified science. The process of trying to reconcile the teachings of Scripture with the tenets of a science which was only 'feeling its way' in the realm of physical phenomena, and which in numerous instances was but 'falsely so-called' ended in theological chaos. Every Church which had left its moorings, lured by the pretensions of the critical school of theology, soon lost all sense of direction and of serious purpose as God's handmaid to minister His Gospel in the world.

The two great delusions which have cast their mesmeric spell over the modern Church are that the Biblical view of man is outmoded by the view of an ascending humanity, and that an all-embracing and advancing science would create 'a social order' that would render obsolete all Christian effort. The idea of 'the ascent of man' with which men like Henry Drummond charmed the ears of a complacent generation is not by any means dead. The irresistible march of science would eventually waylay all the theological bogies of narrow credal statements, and open to man a door of hope more intelligible to his mind than the supernatural way of salvation offered in the Bible!

This growing denial of the fundamental truths of Christian theology and the substitution of 'another gospel' saw the human landslide away from the Church. If the Biblical view of God, man, sin and destiny is wrong then the Church itself is obsolete. So men reasoned. But the Church in the interest of self-preservation would, if it could, retain the people, and this it sought to do by the ingenious but fatal process of adaptation. The Church whose name means 'called out' would now go back to the world out of which it was called. It was no longer 'Come with us' but 'We go with you'.

To retain the interest of the people the Church, as it began to decline, became 'socially minded'. It must, in cheap phrase, 'hike with the hikers', approach the youth on the level of their recreation such as the cinema with its often false presentation of life, and tone down its great message to make it acceptable to that elusive person 'the man in the street.'

This policy of adaptation has been followed to a tragic degree. Its pursuance spells the loss of Christian dignity, and a reversal to the lower levels of worldly conduct. Let me use an illustration. When Abraham asked his servant to seek out a bride for his son, the servant asked a natural question. If the maid proved reluctant to leave her native land, would he bring Isaac down to her country? The answer is significant. 'Beware that thou bring not my son thither again.' God's prince and heir must not so demean himself—or 'go down' to the worldliness and idolatries out of which God had graciously lifted him. It ill becomes the professing Church of God to lower her position to the level of the world, and to bring the very mire of the world into her own royal apartments. Today some churches are nothing but centres of useless activities and entertainments.

'What fellowship has light with darkness?' Through the proclamation of the Gospel and her own holy conduct, the Church should seek to save men by raising them on to her own level; but when she leaves her place to link arms with the world God will disown her. Her present feebleness in the presence of a rising tide of evil is the surest indication that this has happened.

Chapter VII

Technical and political control over nuclear power

THE UNPREDICTABLE STORM AND THE NEW LAMP WHICH FAILED

We mentioned how the Church, generally speaking, linked itself to the chariot of a science which never hesitated to throw scorn on the Bible as a dubious source of knowledge, and on its claim to be the only lamp to show man his way and his destiny. It would never do, however, for men pretending to scholarship to lie buried in the doctrinal obscurantism of a past age. The dawn of a new day hailed man away from those rigid and grotesque theological beliefs which the benighted and unquestioning men of other times accepted in good faith. And what a pity those men of old did not live to enjoy the brighter light conferred on the world by this new revelation!

The writer remembers an 'evangelical campaign' held in a Scottish town over twenty years ago. The preacher on that occasion went on to speak of a 'science which walked by faith' and which would lead mankind into a warless, happy era. Science has certainly 'walked' a good deal since then. Our fear is that it has travelled just a little too far. It has even intruded into Nature's inner chambers and has succeeded both in discovering her great secret, and in disintegrating her very substance. There is nothing more obvious than that this intrusion is resented, and she may yet show her displeasure at man's prying into her heart by reacting in an inconceivably terrible way. Those who have followed the progress of physics are on this point the most apprehensive. The fair country which we looked for has faded out by the sudden appearance of a yawning abyss unrelieved by a ray of light. It is the end of the road. When H. G. Wells ended his literary career with the book *Mind at the End of its Tether* he wrote of the "frightful queerness which has come into life. Even quite unobservant people are betraying a certain wonder that something is happening so that life will never be quite the same again".

The fabrication of the atomic bomb was the outstanding fruit of physical science during the Second World War. The genius of technologists with their formulae which contain everything of which reason is capable, but which have no moral purpose and no worthy end for man to aim at, has provided us with two preliminary flashes of what is in store for us. The men in the laboratories tell us they are not concerned with 'ends' or with moral issues, but with scientific research and progress. Progress is mere 'bulldozing through nature' without any concern that there is no corresponding moral progress or spiritual vision which could prevent abuse of these discoveries. The scientific mind is professedly indifferent to the moral considerations involved, in providing man with catastrophic weapons with which to destroy himself and the world.

Professor A. D. Richie, Edinburgh, in *Science, Civilization and Religion*, explains that the disillusionment we now feel so keenly is due to the neglect of proper moral ends in favour of mere means worked out in the physical sphere. It is as if we had provided ourselves with a high-powered car in which we were to race along an unknown and ill-lit road without asking whether it led to danger or safety. So much for a science intolerant of the Bible and ungoverned by moral considerations. It may be an exaggeration to say so, but mankind is now left in a kind of scientific asylum without any accepted or recognised authority to which it can appeal against the terrible prospects it has created for itself. God's Word of salvation has been rejected as a way out of our difficulties, in favour of a science which can only provide us with an uncertain seat on the brink of a volcanic precipice. Having rejected God's claim upon us we found the atomic bomb.

It was on the 6th day of August, 1945 at 9 o'clock in the evening that these words over the air reached the ears of men. "This revelation of the secrets of Nature, long mercifully withheld from men, should arouse the most solemn reflections in the mind and conscience of every human being capable of comprehension. We must indeed pray that these awful agencies will be made to conduce peace among the nations. . .instead of inflicting immeasurable havoc upon the entire globe. . ."

The words are those of Mr Winston Churchill. They had to do with the atomic bomb which had been dropped that morning on Hiroshima. Earlier in the day President Truman announced that "Man has succeeded in harnessing the basic power of the universe—from which the sun itself derives its power".

From distant Tokyo came the words, "Nearly all living things have perished. The dead are burnt beyond recognition. The destruction. . .is indescribable".

An airman remote from the scene said, "We heard the roar of the bomb, and the column of smoke and fire arose to ten miles"

What is this atomic power which is so fraught with possibilities for the weal or woe of man? While even physical science itself recognises the ultimate mystery associated with this dread discovery, ordinary people are unlikely to understand those tiny, invisible atomic worlds, with their strange resemblance to solar systems in the greater realm of astronomy.

[*What follows is an impressionistic, rather than systematic, account.* :-Ed.]

Atoms are not solid but consist mostly of space. Their heaviest part, called the 'nucleus', is at the centre. In close proximity and comparatively quiescent are fundamental particles such as 'protons'. At some distance from the nucleus, other particles called 'electrons' fly around these quieter protons at possibly the speed of light or about 11,000,000 miles a minute. An electron revolves millions of times around the proton in one second. And the distance between the nucleus and the electron planet is as great in proportion as the distance between our earth and the sun. To disconcert and disintegrate this astonishing 'merry-go-round' world, it is necessary to attack it with free electrons, driven by a force equivalent to a million volts. In order to prevent an escape of those electrons every precaution is taken to keep them within the strong walls of what are called cyclotropes. No one can predetermine what their escape might mean. What would happen if these hitherto well-managed atomic energies broke away from their well-guarded 'cages' and seized upon subatomic forces in the external world?

Many scientists have expressed their fear that a slight lapse at some unguarded moment might start a catastrophe of such dimensions as man never imagined. Once a 'chain' combination is established between atomic and subatomic forces no power that man can think of could prevent continents being torn up and thrown in angry fury into the roaring stratosphere. Such an explosion would create a pressure wave which in its turn would start a wind of fire travelling at up to 1,000 miles an hour.

The latest conclusion of science is that this is a distinct possibility. This very admission is agreeable to God's Word which warns us that the world at last shall pass away 'with a great noise' and the elements 'shall melt with fervent heat'. How solemn it is to think that the astronomical universe in the last analysis came into being by that 'word of power' by which God created all things.

The significant and awe-inspiring fact which emerges, as it appears to us now, is that the power which resided in the creative word or will of the Most High adhered to the universe and became an ingredient in it.

A more terrifying fact is the discovery that 99.9 per cent of the mass of matter in the universe is fire energy related to the atom. In the words of Professor Albert Einstein it is like a set fire ready for the match to light it. This is the power with which man is playing, and which he is trying to unleash or harness to his bidding.

Recently the writer was introduced to a book entitled *Must Destruction be our Destiny?* by Dr H. Brown of the Institute for Nuclear Studies at Chicago University. This is the work of an expert in his own province. The book is 'dedicated to humanity in the hope that it may exist longer than recent events would lead us to suppose'. The learned Doctor sent an autographed copy of his book to 'sweet Christine' from the Scottish Highlands, in the hope that she might know 'what we are heading for'. He may have realised that the prospects of youth were often brighter than they are today. May the merciful God preserve every child from these potential horrors!

In this book we have a cool survey of the prospects of civilisation 'should no lock be found to close the door' against the potential destruction to come, and no key to open it once it is locked. The relevant fact is that at the present moment a bomb could be produced many times more powerful than the comparative snowflake—'the first crude bomb'—which was dropped on Hiroshima. By sober calculation it is estimated that given a sufficient concentration of human beings one of these could kill five million human beings. A large and powerful nation could be destroyed in hours. The next War would possibly come without warning, to avoid speedy or simultaneous retaliation. The psychological effects of atomic warfare are unpredictable. Left without defence amid 'sudden destruction' a 'great fear' would produce a state of mind better left to the imagination. In a few years atomic supremacy will have no significance, and soon war could be waged at a cost equal to the money we spent in ten days in the Second World War. At present, however, the nations are spending about £7,000,000,000 on weapons of war.

Dr Brown gives a lurid picture of a large city bombed, where nothing could be done from within or without to help. A saturation quantity of bombs would produce world chaos.

Would a nation at war use this weapon? The answer is that a nation at war uses all its weapons. It was not through any feelings of humanity or fear of retaliation that poison gas was not used in the last War, but because gas was far from being 'a decisive weapon'. Adolf Hitler used it where it could be decisive. More than five million human beings were made to pass through his gas chambers and crematoria.

Is there any physical defence against this power? One suggestion is that large cities should move underground to a depth of about one mile. The one objection to this idea is that an enemy could easily walk into this gigantic hole with 'an atomic egg' in his pocket. 'Death in such a subterranean city would be a dread experience', says the learned scientist. And as the world is run today the dispersal of mankind into 'the wide open spaces' of the earth is impractical.

To the scientific mind there is only one other hope: the immediate and voluntary unification of mankind in one great international state in which the recognised authorities would control and veto this weapon and other potential means of destruction. The moral resources of mankind should be pooled in the interests of preservation. The ideologies which lacerate the world should be scrapped, and men should come together in a great world-brotherhood.

In this book there is, needless to say, no word about God, His eternal laws, the abounding iniquity of the times, and the wrath of God revealed from Heaven against all unrighteousness of men. It is literally a godless book.

In this country a similar view of our prospects is taken by the scientific mind. Professor E. L. Woodward, Oxford, in his pamphlet *Some Political Consequences of the Atomic Bomb*, is sombre to the verge of hopeless pessimism. Because he sees no door of hope for man at present he asks the question, "Will the *Dies Irae* be chanted by a generation without faith and without hope, and will man find himself walking on an ever-darkening road singing dismally,

To-morrow, and to-morrow, and to-morrow. . .
And all our yesterdays have lighted fools the way
To dusty death"?

Professor Albert Einstein does not pin his faith so much on the moral sense of mankind as on the task of educating the nations on the dangers ahead. The following is a letter of appeal addressed to his wealthy friends throughout the United States.

I write to you for help at the suggestion of a friend.

Through the release of atomic energy, our generation has brought into the world the most revolutionary force since prehistoric man's discovery of fire. This basic power of the universe cannot be fitted into the out-moded concept of narrow nationalisms.

For there is no secret and there is no defence, there is no possibility of control, except through the aroused understanding and insistence of the peoples of all nations. We scientists recognise the inescapable responsibility to carry to our fellow-citizens an understanding of the simple facts of atomic energy and their implications for society.

We need $1,000,000 for this great educational task. I do not hesitate to call upon you to help.

The undertone of this letter is like an S.O.S. sent out at the approach of an unpredictable storm. But what a tragedy that an Israelite, and one of the world's greatest minds, should look to 'the arm of flesh' instead of calling men back to the God Who alone is a shield to the nations which obey Him.

If the scientific world is therefore apprehensive about the future of man it is because it knows that the gathering clouds on the horizon are loaded with sore and great trouble for this world.

Chapter VIII

Impending conflagration

CAN WE SURVIVE?

It would be both unfair and wrong to deprecate the attitude of those eminent men to this problem. No doubt a strong moral approach to this whole question of 'to be or not to be' could be most useful. But is it possible to initiate a strong moral movement in the world as it is now? If genuine morality has its sources in the Christian Gospel it is doubtful, one fears, whether the nations have the necessary moral resources to resist any major danger of this kind. If the nations are destitute of Christian morality how can they offer effectual and righteous opposition to such potential dangers?

Let us for a moment look at the moral situation as it obtains, not at the ends of the earth, but on our own British hearth. We still cling, perhaps with a touch of pride, to the phrase, 'this Christian nation'. Doubtless there are still found among us evidences of former greatness and those rare qualities which could only thrive in a true Christian environment. We are looking at the moral and spiritual complexion of a nation not considered the worst.

Where do we stand? One had almost said—Where do we lie? The appalling and revealing figures which are supplied from time to time with reference to the moral state of the nation prove that in a very literal sense the words, 'an adulterous generation' are not inapplicable. And in these times such sins are largely a hidden plague because the means to hide them are available. Only One Eye can see the whole.

The charge that Britain is a drunken nation is perhaps an exaggeration; but when one considers the astronomical figures representing the money spent on drink we cannot tell whether the charge is not true. If the world is at present spending 7,000 million pounds on war preparations, Britain spends 680 million pounds on its drink bill. It is criminal beyond words that in these days of world hunger, mountains of grain and sugar which should go to an emaciated race should be thrown into the distillers' swill. It is beyond the power of man to understand what immeasurable sorrows follow in the wake of this brutal trade. There are few vices which disintegrate personality like this; for its effect too often is to debase its victim to the level of the subhuman.

Other evils are even more pronounced. The nation is swarming with covetous idlers whose sole occupation is to infect with the gambling virus the minds of the rising generation. If this evil is in danger of touching the very steps of the throne little wonder though the imitative and unreflecting masses should consider it 'the thing to do'. It is this fever of covetousness which lies behind the growing dishonesties which are such an ominous symptom of our age. During the past year there have been 120,000 cases of burglary and housebreaking recorded in our Criminal Courts. From the young pagan who watches the uninhabited house, or who stalks an old woman in the twilight for the sake of her purse, to the deep 'black market' intriguer, the nation is slowly sinking in a sea of crime.

The growing moral disintegration has produced two things. There is on the one hand a restless pursuit of 'pleasure'. For example, in the City of Glasgow over New Year's week 1948, cinemas, dance halls and theatres netted £300,000. On the other hand there is a growing impatience with every voice that would recall the nation to a higher moral standard. Those who attempt to do this are labelled either Puritan obscurantists, or fossils left over from 'the age of Calvinism' or Victorian conventions.

Very few places on this earth were more renowned for their piety than our Scottish Highlands less than a century ago. In those days the youth of our Highlands, in many instances, spent part of their time building 'Meeting Houses' in which they could worship God. And it was considered no hardship to walk many miles over stream and moorland to hear the Gospel on the Lord's Day. This thirst for the Word of God is a thing of the past. Nowadays they travel up to 50 miles to attend a dance, while in many instances the Church is looked upon as 'a place for old folk'. This however is a universal state of things fostered by the false and fatal view of life given by many broadcasters and by the emergent hedonistic paganism of Hollywood. The Local Government Bill before Parliament contains provisions for expenditure by the local authority for entertainment in theatres and licensed dance halls. This disastrous innovation shows how the cold, ill winds of godlessness are rising.

How then can such a nation as this pool its moral resources? From what pure, invigorating springs can these be drawn? If we say that there is no hope, it is because history is an everlasting proof that where the carcase lies, there the eagles gather. In other words we become a prey to destructive forces because we have already suffered a moral death.

We already said something about the decline of the Church. The question is often asked—Why is the Church so ambiguous and timid in its message, and so feeble in its action? The story in the Gospel of the parent who came with his afflicted child— the victim of demonic power—to our Lord's disciples that they might heal him is apposite here. When, in all the dignity of their office, they stood before the evil spirit they were helpless. Their voice carried no authority, and their hand carried no power. These constituted the Church. 'Why could not we cast him out?' Our communities in these times are the abode of foul spirits in whose presence official Christianity is powerless. The startling truth is that to-day some Churches seem to have ceased to be interested either in the spiritual redemption of men or in the preservation of that Gospel by which man can be redeemed. In proof of this we have only to look, for example, at the puerilities of Anglo-Catholicism in the English Church, or the literature of the Iona Community in the Scottish Church.

Many Christian people are alarmed today because they find that when a stand is made for the Bible as an infallible Revelation, for the observance of the Lord's Day, for the Reformed faith with its exposure of error and proclamation of truth, or for the defence of Christian existence itself, a large percentage of Christian ministers seem, like Gallio of old, to 'care for none of these things', not even in the interest of self-preservation. And we fear the reason is a lack of any experience of the redeeming grace of God in their own lives.

Not so long ago the writer listened to a theological professor of international reputation, who teaches in one of the largest Colleges in the world. He admitted that what he feared more than anything was that many of the young men, prospective ministers of the Church, who sat on the benches before him, had no saving knowledge of God. Let us make no mistake here. When a Church is ruled by such men God will leave it, and another will take possession. When this happens the end is at hand.

An insight into the mind and spiritual discernment of the Churches is afforded by such pamphlets as *The Era of Atomic Power* by the British Council of Churches. Here the whole insistence is laid on 'the evil of war and the atomic bomb'. Next to nothing is said about the moral and spiritual background of physical violence. The cause of war is ignored, while the effects are deplored. Fallen man, indeed, does grieve over the effects of sin, but seldom over sin itself. The Churches in the Report are more anxious to fit their pronouncement with 'the British way of life', or to find out whether they should embarrass the government by declaring their opposition to the use of the bomb in any future war. That is all, and comment is useless.

Another book, *Atomic Warfare and the Christian Faith*, issued by the Federal Council of the Churches of Christ in America, speaks in similar tones, not of grief for sin, but of regret that 'Christian nations' should have followed a policy of obliteration-bombing in Europe and Japan.

We already referred to the Roman Catholic pronouncement in *God and the Atom*. Here we have a self-drawn portrayal of the modern Church following uncertainly in the wake of political issues and undecided whether it should say this or that in the guarded language of diplomacy. But the prophetic voice of true Christian witness begins with, 'Thus saith the Lord'. It begins there because the Bible is eternally explicit and authoritative, as well as eternally appropriate to every problem affecting mankind in the sphere of what ought or ought not to be.

'It is not lawful for thee to have her' was the word of Christ's prophet to the earthly power. For uttering that word, he lost his head, but having kept the faith he won the approval of the Christian conscience to the end of time.

The reply given by the Quaker Body to these reports makes the observation that when 'the Church is not prophetic it will sink below the level of the politicians who are dealing with human nature on a different plane'. This has happened.

Some, impatient with all institutional religion as inapplicable to the present situation, would pin their hopes on the rising generation. The efforts which are being made both in this country and in America 'to bring the youth to Christ' are those of earnest and good men. Let us look for the facts, however. Take, for example, the pamphlet issued by the Church Council entitled *Religion and the Forces*. Here we get a very intimate and near view of the attitude and outlook of our youth with regard to the Bible, the Person of our Lord, the moral law, the Church, what constitutes Christianity, and what is a Christian. The leaflet gives the word 'Christian' a very wide and undefined significance; but even by stretching its sympathy and charity so far it has to admit that 'convinced Churchmen' (not Christians!) are few. The general attitude of the youth to religion is 'at best indifferent, and at worst hostile'. Whether hostility to the things of God is worse than indifference is a point we are not concerned to settle. The value of the leaflet consists in showing that the mind of our youth is largely destitute of Christian knowledge, through influences other than those which flow from the Christian Gospel. We are in the presence of a form of paganism which is intolerant both of Gospel and Law as revealed. Allowing that it is usual for the passing generation to think less of youth than of themselves, those who are in close touch with the rising generation are deeply apprehensive as to what the world of tomorrow, in which they are to rule, will be like. That a vicious paganism is maturing before our very eyes we feel in the moral atmosphere of the times. None needs our protection and prayers more than our children.

Is it possible to get even a closer view of the world as it is? To say that a cloud of evil is over this planet is trite. We are in the presence of something even more ominous.

It was about the year 1874 that the Russian writer Fyodor Dostoyevski gave his 'Reflections' to his contemporaries. Unlike many in those days of shallow optimism and insipid humanism, this man warned Europe of a coming disaster. He lived in a time of superficial progress in the political and material sphere; but he saw the unhinging of civilisation in the continued atheism of France, the morbid scepticism of Germany with its wild attacks on Christian theology and morality, in the dangerous and irrelevant bluff of so-called 'Catholic Christianity', and in the fatal illusion of moral progress. He believed moral disintegration was rapidly overtaking Europe. Knowing 'what is in man' he warned his contemporaries that they were living in a fool's paradise, blind to the fact that the very foundations of all order, peace and safety were breaking up. The ferocious instincts of fallen man, however much concealed by the illusion of culture, and momentarily kept in subjection by our conventional civilisation, can only be controlled by the grace of God. The outbreak will be terrible beyond all knowledge when it comes. Man is a wild beast who nurses in his heart desperate wickedness which only the power of God can dislodge. Without some such radical change there is no hope of world survival.

As it is, men are carelessly approaching the edge of an abyss unaware that the intangible link preventing them from falling in has been removed by disorderly lust, lawless conduct, intellectual blindness, and spiritual anarchy. An evil heart of unbelief with regard to the nature of God, the Word of God, and what He has both threatened and promised to do, is the final cause of man's destruction.

There may still exist a thin cord linking our earthly order with the eternal order above the world. This 'cord' is the presence, prayers and obedience of those 'fools for Christ's sake' who continue, in fear and humility, to acknowledge God's sovereignty and supremacy, and the utter dependence of the creature upon His mercy. This idea of a 'thin cord' is another way of saying that unless the Lord had left us 'a very small remnant' we had 'been as Sodom and been made like unto Gomorrah'. It is a revealed truth that without the presence of God's people the world could not last for one hour. What some fear is that the last strands in this last thin cord, between a guilty world and God's long-suffering mercy, are breaking away.

The time will never come, however great the darkness, when God will not have His witnesses. 'They shall fear Thee as long as the sun and the moon endure, throughout all generations.' Let us remember, however, that God did destroy by fire the two tiny villages of Sodom and Gomorrah notwithstanding the presence of 'just Lot' among them. God's controversy with us is far deeper than it was with those heathen, who lived in the dim twilight of a shadowy dispensation. They had only the light of Nature. We have 'the true Light which gives light to every man that comes into the world'. The aggravation is therefore infinitely greater; for judgment will be measured out in proportion to privilege. 'This is the condemnation, that light is come into the world, and men loved darkness rather than light because their deeds were evil.' If Israel had heeded the divine warning against closing the door of hope on themselves they would not have passed through the fire and agonies of yesterday and today. *[This might seem to blame the Holocaust on its victims. Given the context, however, it is instead a forewarning of fierce judgement. :-Ed.]* "If we sin wilfully after that we have received the knowledge of the truth there remains no more sacrifice for sins, but a certain fearful looking-for of judgment and fiery indignation, which shall devour the adversaries." 'For our God is a consuming fire.'

We shall leave it to God's providence, as it shall unfold itself in the awe-inspiring events of the coming days, to fulfil

His own prophetic Word before the eyes of apostate nations. "And I will show wonders in Heaven above and signs in the earth beneath; blood, fire and vapour of smoke: the sun shall be turned into darkness, and the moon into blood before the great and notable day of the Lord." It is both solemn and significant that these words were repeated by the apostle Peter on the Day of Pentecost after the Lord had poured out His Spirit on 'every nation under heaven' representatively present at Jerusalem. They serve to show what dire judgments would come upon the earth when men rejected and quenched God's Spirit and Gospel blessings. The prophets and apostles, like their Lord, all foresaw the darkness and 'distress of nations' which would truly follow this rejection of God and His grace. If we despise the only 'sign' given by God in the death and resurrection of His dear Son then we must endure to see other 'signs'. 'Beware, therefore, lest that come upon you which is spoken of in the prophets: Behold, ye despisers, and wonder and perish. . .' (*Acts* 13: 40)

It would be wrong to end on a note of despair. Beyond these tribulations and through the vista of prophetic time, in the light of God's promise, we are given a glimpse of the fair prospect of the Church of God in the world.

As the prophet Jeremiah in symbolic vision saw, through 'the vapour of smoke' issuing from the seething cauldron, the blossoming almond tree of a new spring, we also may see on the distant landscape and beyond, the 'signs' which the Lord will show—the blossoming Tree of Promise which proclaims the beginning of a new day—the long happy summer of millennial peace awaiting the people of God.

That day will come through the prayers of God's people for the promised outpourings of the Holy Spirit, and through the faithful preaching of the glorious Gospel which is the power of God unto Salvation.

'Even so, come, Lord Jesus.' In the stormy days which lie ahead of us the Church of Christ itself shall be shown 'hard things' and given to drink 'the wine of astonishment'. Some of

God's servants in the past, when they pleaded on their knees the promised day of millennial blessedness, could not endure to think of the tribulations which would precede that longed-for day. It is God's intention to bring His people Home through both 'fire and water', but in every furnace they shall suffer no hurt, for beside them stands One Whose form is like the Son of God.

Publications of The Revd Murdoch Campbell, M.A. (1900-1974)

God's Unsettled Controversy (London, circa 1944)
Thy Own Soul Also <u>or</u> *The Crisis in the Church* (Glasgow 1945)
The King's Friend (Glasgow 1946)
The Coming Storm (Glasgow 1948, reprinted 2016)
Gleanings of Highland Harvest (1953, 1954, 1957, 1964, 1989, 2016)
The Diary of Jessie Thain (1955)
The Loveliest Story Ever Told (Inverness 1962; reprinted 2016)
In All Their Affliction (Inverness 1967; reprinted 1969, 1987, 2003)
Everlasting Love: Devotional Sermons (Edinburgh: Knox Press 1968)
From Grace to Glory: Meditations on the Book of Psalms (Banner of Truth Trust 1970)
No Night There: Devotional Sermons (Stornoway 1972)
Memories of a Wayfaring Man (Inverness 1974; reprinted 2016)
Tobraichean Solais: Wells of Joy (Covenanters Press 2013)
The Suburbs of Heaven: the Diary of Murdoch Campbell (Covenanters Press 2014)

Translations

Des Konings Vriend: Het leven en sterven Norman Macdonald (C. B. van Woerden Jr te Akkrum, Utrecht 1961)
Herinneringen van een Pelgrim (trs. J. Kooistra, Veenendaal 1978)
Dagboek van Jessie Thain (J. Kooistra 1980)
Nalezingen van de Highland-oogst (J. Kooistra, Gorinchem 1995)
In al hun benauwdheid: pastorale memoires van een Schotse predikant (trs. Ruth Pieterman: Gouda 2013)

Pamphlets

The Earth-bound Vision: A Critical Examination of
    Pre-millennialism
After Bishops – What? The New Peril
Christians and the Use of Nuclear Weapons

Tract

When my Heart Smiled

Acknowledgements

Thanks to Derek Prescott for photographic work. Special thanks to my wife Evie for her suggestions and forbearance.

David Campbell
Strachur 2016

Lightning Source UK Ltd.
Milton Keynes UK
UKOW05f1345081116
287148UK00001B/36/P